THE 100 GREATEST TV SHOWS OF ALL TIME

CONTENTS

6 TOP 20

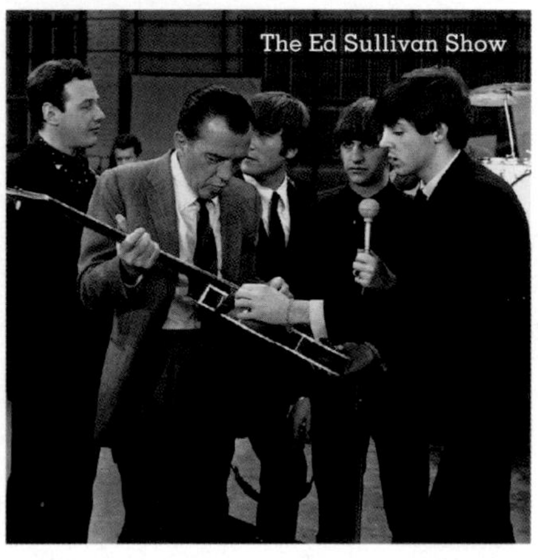
The Ed Sullivan Show

Taxi

44 COMEDIES

70 GAME SHOWS

Wheel of Fortune

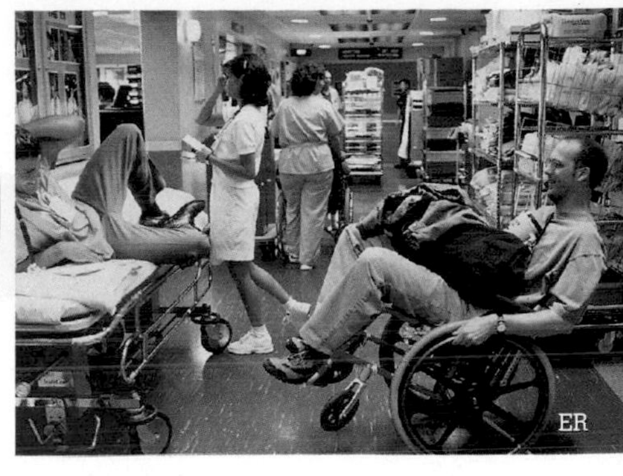

ER

The Carol Burnett Show

Charlie's Angels

Special thanks to Anna Yelenskaya

Published by Entertainment Weekly Books, a division of Time Inc. Home Entertainment, 1271 Avenue of the Americas, New York, NY 10020

ISBN: 1-883013-42-9

Library of Congress Catalog Card Number: 98-85634

We welcome your comments and suggestions about Entertainment Weekly Books. Please write us at: Entertainment Weekly Books, Attention: Book Editors, PO Box 11016, Des Moines, IA 50336-1016. If you would like to order additional copies of any of our books, please call 800-327-6388 (Monday through Friday, 7 a.m. to 8 p.m., or Saturday, 7 a.m. to 6 p.m., central time).

Mary Tyler Moore and Dick Van Dyke warming up *The Dick Van Dyke Show*'s audience

THE TOP 20

IN 1938, AFTER ATTENDING A LAB DEMONSTRATION of the nascent television technology, writer E.B. White wrote the following in *Harper's* magazine: "I believe television is going to be the test of the modern world, and that in this new opportunity...we shall discover either a new and unbearable disturbance of the general peace or a saving radiance in the sky. We shall stand or fall by television—of that I am quite sure." ✦ Prescient words, especially coming from the guy who wrote *Charlotte's Web*. The funny thing is, both sides of White's either-or forecast have come true. "A new and unbearable disturbance of the general peace"? Sounds like *World Championship Wrestling* to us. "A saving radiance in the sky"? That could be images of Tiananmen Square broadcast around the planet, or *Sesame Street* beamed into the home of an inner-city child. Far more than the "test of the modern world," television has become our shallow, bright, and primary canvas of expression. ✦ The top 20 TV shows celebrated in this chapter, then, are more than just monuments in the pop landscape. They're part of who we are and how we reference reality. Some of the shows here have served as blueprints for the very way stories are told. Over the course of its 20-year run, *Gunsmoke* set the conventions of how "Old West" communities are portrayed. *The Ed Sullivan Show* was the variety format, period, full stop. *All in the Family* brokered a new frankness in TV characterization, while *The Mary Tyler Moore Show* established the grammar of the ensemble workplace comedy that *Cheers* would refine and perfect. *Dallas* ushered in an era of camp seriousness in prime-time drama (*Melrose Place* would be unthinkable without it), while *Hill Street Blues* brought new complexities and shadings to the heroic-professional genre (*ER* would be unthinkable without it). ✦ Often these shows broke the rules only to refashion the mainstream in their image. *I Love Lucy* had any number of strikes against it going in: a female star who'd never really made it in movies, an ethnic husband, a production format (film) and location (Hollywood) that went against the prevailing norm (live and in New York). No matter: After three years at No. 1, *Lucy* was the norm. Decades later, the anomaly was *Seinfeld*, a New York–based comedy of (bad) manners whose sit-around-the-coffee-shop anomie only *felt* live. It ended its nine-year run surrounded by sitcoms huffing and puffing to imitate its evanescent cynicism. ✦ Other shows in this chapter were more subversive, either in intent or in practice. *The Honeymooners* was a blue-collar yawp at the Eisenhower blandness of '50s TV. With *The Twilight Zone*, Rod Serling used sci-fi and horror to tackle themes that censors had blue-penciled out of his serious teleplays. *Star Trek* sneaked similar messages into its scripts and created cult TV in the bargain. *M*A*S*H* was a sitcom that sometimes shunned the laugh track, a boffo antiwar tract that never mentioned Vietnam. *The Simpsons* is a cartoon that's far more deeply—and comically—aware of our modern world than any news show, and *The X-Files* goes so far as to suggest that subversion has become the mainstream. ✦ So, pace E.B. White, we seem to have both stood and fallen by TV. If the medium has rarely lived up to its potential as a positive, enriching social force (and exactly how much C-SPAN do you watch?), the entertainment we have "settled for" has transformed our culture nevertheless—for good, for ill, forever. —TY BURR

PHOTOGRAPH BY NOLA LÓPEZ

AN ALL-STAR CAST AND FIRST-RATE WRITING MADE 'MTM' THE CAT'S MEOW

THE MARY TYLER MOORE SHOW

AS CONCEIVED BY CREATORS James L. Brooks and Allan Burns, Mary Richards was supposed to be a divorcée. But in greenlighting this vehicle for Mary Tyler Moore's post-*Dick Van Dyke Show* return to sitcoms, CBS brass nixed that idea—viewers wouldn't stand for a divorced woman (and some would be confused, thinking Mary had left Van Dyke's Rob Petrie). It was unwarranted cowardice on the network's part—but it set the bar even higher for Brooks, Burns, and Moore; they had to imbue this straight, single "liberated" career woman in her 30s with enough strength, personality, and imagination to avoid (at the dawn of the '70s, when feminism still, after all, had made few inroads in prime time) making her either a lonely spinster or Lucille Ball's in-the-closet lesbian daughter. ✦ What resulted, improbably enough, was the best-written and best-acted show of its era—and arguably the most beloved TV series of all time. *The Mary Tyler Moore Show* came to define the "workplace family" sitcom: Mary labored long hours as an associate producer at the struggling Minneapolis TV station WJM and spent much of her time with her grumpy but paternal boss, Lou Grant (Edward Asner); her wisecracking, brotherly colleague Murray Slaughter (Gavin MacLeod); and the daffy, self-important anchorman Ted Baxter (Ted Knight). Of course, she had another family at home, where she socialized and commiserated with acerbic but sisterly upstairs neighbor Rhoda (Valerie Harper) and their nosy, dithery landlady, Phyllis (Cloris Leachman), who often functioned as the sort of meddling mother-in-law Mary Richards never had. ✦ Within the context of this extended family, Mary led a rich, complex emotional life. Seen from one angle, it was full of disappointments (her romances, some of which lasted for episodes on end, invariably concluded with Mary alone). But viewed another way—the way millions of fans saw her—Mary was surrounded by funny, solid friends who enabled (even "enabled" in its current, pop-psychological sense) her to be happy in her wall-to-wall shag-rug apartment and her wall-to-wall nutty newsroom. ✦ As the series proceeded, things occasionally occurred to threaten the delicate balance of friendship and workplace calm, as when, late in *MTM*'s run, Mary asked Lou out on a date. The episode was fraught wth the tension of taboo—why, Lou was Mary's surrogate *dad*! How could she (or he) feel, uh, you know, *romantic* about the other?! The evening proved to be a comic disaster, of course, filled with funny embarrassment, but at the end of the episode, as always, the workplace-family roles were firmly reestablished and order restored. ✦ Brooks went on to explore the profoundly mixed emotions that exist at our jobs when he wrote and directed the 1987 feature film *Broadcast News*; there, Holly Hunter was a more driven, far less happy Mary Richards. But for television, this Mary was just the one we wanted to see on a Saturday night—a night when many of us might be as dateless and vaguely lonely as Mary herself. So appealing were her fellow players that *MTM* spawned spin-offs galore—*Rhoda, Phyllis,* and, most surprisingly, *Lou Grant*, an hour-long drama in which Asner played the same character straight, as a crusading newspaper editor. But for the comfort and the laughs she gave us, Mary Richards was the character we clung to most fiercely, most loyally. She was, ultimately, the one most worthy of our devotion. —KEN TUCKER

JUST THE FACTS

THE MARY TYLER MOORE SHOW

YEARS ON AIR
1970–77

TOP NIELSEN CHARTING
7th (1972–73)

EMMYS WON
27

WHAT THE NETWORK WANTED CBS asked for (but didn't get) an assurance that Mary would wed in the first season.

QUEL SCANDALE
Mary had sex! Several episodes alluded obliquely to the fact that she sometimes spent the night with a date, and one let slip that she took birth-control pills.

PRODUCTION NOTES
Mary's shoulder-length dark hair in early episodes is actually a wig.

WHAT DID THEY KNOW?
An early TIME magazine review called the show "a disaster for the old co-star of *The Dick Van Dyke Show*. She plays an inadvertent career girl, jilted by the rounder she put through medical school, and working as a 'gofer' at a Minneapolis TV station. Her bosses...do an injustice to even the worst of local TV news."

ORIGINAL CASTING
MacLeod was originally considered for the Lou Grant role.

ORIGINAL CHARACTERS
Ted Baxter was first visualized as a potential love interest for Mary. It was only after Knight was cast that Baxter was transformed into a dim-witted stuffed shirt.

NO CREDIT WHERE IT'S DUE Murray was the only member of the newsroom staff never to win the fictional Teddy award; MacLeod was the only regular cast member never to win an Emmy.

PRESCIENT CASTING
A young Helen Hunt played Murray's daughter in a seventh-season episode in which Murray ghostwrites a newspaper article for Ted that earns wide acclaim; Henry Winkler, fresh out of Yale drama school, appeared as a dinner guest of Mary's.

CAMEOS
Among the famous faces that popped up were Walter Cronkite's and Betty Ford's. Among the famous voices was Johnny Carson's; he actually showed at one of Mary's infamously awful parties—but (just her luck) only after the lights went out.

JUST THE FACTS

SEINFELD

YEARS ON AIR
1990–98
(pilot aired in 1989)

TOP NIELSEN CHARTING
1st (1994–95)

EMMYS WON
11

GROUNDBREAKING MOMENT
Entire episode about masturbation ("The Contest"), in which the word was never once used

ORIGINAL TITLE
The Seinfeld Chronicles

REPLACEMENT PARTS
Barney Martin replaced Phil Burns as Mort Seinfeld; Jerry Stiller replaced John Randolph as Frank Costanza. (Randolph's scenes were reshot–a TV rarity–by Stiller for syndication.)

ORIGINAL CONCEPT
The original idea was about a stand-up comedian and how everyday situations supply the material that ends up in his monologue. When the characters and the situations started getting more laughs than the monologue, they became the center of the show.

WHAT DID THEY KNOW?
"This five-episode summer diversion, which NBC has been kicking around for at least half a season waiting for the 'right time' to unleash on the viewing public, is not what could be termed an inspired piece of television."
–*The Washington Times*, May 31, 1990

OF ALL THE FUNNY PHRASES ASSOCIATED WITH '**SEINFELD**'—"yada, yada, yada," "master of your domain," "sponge-worthy"—one of the funniest has to be "too New York, too Jewish." That's what dubious NBC execs pronounced when they first saw Jerry Seinfeld's sitcom back in 1989. Ha-ha! Shows you what they knew: nothing. ✦ *Seinfeld*, that brilliantly self-reflexive series about a stand up comic and his three pals, went on to become the defining sitcom for the '90s. In its eight years on the air, *Seinfeld* changed the tone of TV, our Thursday-night plans, the way we talk. It spawned enough imitators to fill Yankee Stadium, boosted sales of Jujyfruits and Binaca, and even made medical history—a journal reported that a Massachusetts fan laughed so hard, he kept fainting. It made a mint for NBC—and not a junior one either. ✦ Still, you can understand why network execs had their jitters. Created by clean-cut stand-up Jerry and surly genius Larry David, *Seinfeld* was not only

SEINFELD

2

New York-centric, but extremely unorthodox. The four emotionally stunted pals—whiny Elaine (Julia Louis-Dreyfus), human cartoon Kramer (Michael Richards), sublimely neurotic George (Jason Alexander), and relative straight man Jerry—spent hours of expensive network airtime dissecting the inane minutiae of everyday life: How the second button is the most important on the shirt (if it's too high, "you look like you live with your mother"). How to get a table at a Chinese restaurant. Why funerals are a good place to take dates ("It's a golden opportunity to advance the relationship," said Jerry. "She's crying—you put your arms around her"). ✦ That last tidbit hints at another *Seinfeld* innovation: Never had TV been so gleefully soulless. Even Archie was a bigot with a heart of gold. But this foursome had iced Snapple in their veins. Commitment-phobe Jerry dumped women nearly every episode—one for having man hands, another for eating peas one at a time. Elaine was, as Louis-Dreyfus once said, "a miserable, decrepit old wretch [who] should have her tubes tied." George rejoiced when his fiancée died. Only Kramer, the high-haired wackball who didn't know the meaning of the word doorbell, had half a conscience, more invasive than truly selfish. ✦ Over the years, the quartet broke tube taboo after taboo, mocking deaf people, cancer, football-shaped goiters, and mental retardation. Even masturbation and oral sex slipped onto the airwaves, thinly disguised with masterful euphemisms. ✦ Not exactly safe, family, Tony Danza-type television. But it was precisely *Seinfeld*'s shocking deviations from formula that separated it from the sea of tapioca. The show gave us a peek at our Jungian dark shadow. It let nothing—not feelings, not death—get in the way of a punchline. ✦ Granted, the last couple of years were somewhat of a letdown. *Seinfeld*'s trademark four plots—which would always weave seamlessly together—veered toward Carrot Top wackiness. Kramer importing Cubans? C'mon. And the final episode—where Jerry and Co. get sent to jail for their callousness—taught us an unnecessary lesson. ✦ But even at its worst, *Seinfeld* was as energizing as a bowl of Rice Krispies. Too New York, too Jewish? Yeah. And *The Godfather* was too Italian. —A.J. JACOBS/PHOTOGRAPH BY JULIE DENNIS

A SHOW ABOUT NOTHING?
NOW THAT WAS SOMETHING!

"STIFLE IT!" HE SAID—BUT THE LAUGHS KEPT COMING HARDER

AT 9:30 P.M. ON TUESDAY, Jan. 12, 1971, CBS aired the following disclaimer: "The program you are about to see is *All in the Family*. It seeks to throw a humorous spotlight on our frailties, prejudices, and concerns. By making them a source of laughter, we hope to show—in a mature fashion—just how absurd they are." ✦ What followed was like nothing that had ever been seen on American television. In that first episode, paterfamilias Archie Bunker was like a verbal Gatling gun, firing off nonstop gripes about "spades, spics, and hebes." When he and "dingbat" wife Edith came home from church early, with Archie denouncing the sermon as "socialist propaganda," they interrupted their daughter and son-in-law doing the wild thing. ("11:10 on Sunday morning?" Archie bellowed.) ✦ CBS hunkered down for the onslaught of expected complaints, even hiring extra operators to field angry calls. This, despite the fact that the network hadn't really publicized the show (not even a plot summary in *TV Guide*) and had buried it in a graveyard time slot right before a struggling series called *60 Minutes*. Strangely, what CBS was most worried about was the sexual reference—not offending viewers' ethnic sensibilities. Up to an hour before airtime, network execs had argued with creator-producer Norman Lear and his partner, Bud Yorkin, that a milder episode should be broadcast. Lear and Yorkin threatened to quit, and CBS blinked. ✦ Lear had come up with the idea for the show in 1967, when he learned of a British sitcom, *Till Death Do Us Part*, about an unregenerate working-class bigot; he acquired the U.S. rights and created an American version, drawing heavily on his own father ("a Jewish Archie Bunker," he said) for the lead. Little did he know that his show would hit like a tornado of fresh air sweeping through a prime-time landscape blotted by the likes of *Love, American Style* and *Hee Haw*. ✦ Though that first episode didn't do well in the Nielsens, by September, *All In the Family* had risen to No. 1, where it would remain for five more years. Along the way, it raised issues that had never been even glancingly referred to in a prime-time sitcom, much less mined for humor. Like politics: "Lemme tell you about Richard E. Nixon," Archie ranted at one point. "He knows how to keep his wife Pat home. Roosevelt could never do that with Eleanor." Or religion: When a neighbor observed that the names of Archie's parents suggested he might be Jewish, he answered: "David and Sarah, two names right out of the Bible, which has got nothing to do with the Jews." ✦ Neither did *All In the Family* avoid deeply personal subjects. In the sixth episode, Gloria's pregnancy ended in a miscarriage; later, America watched as Edith tried to cope with menopause (Archie grumbled in exasperation that he'd give her exactly 30 seconds to get through her "change of life"). Breast cancer, impotence, Mike's vasectomy—the list goes on and on. ✦ It would be nice to think that the show helped change the world (Lear dismisses this notion out of hand), or at least changed television. But old habits die hard. When CBS aired a 20th-anniversary tribute to the show, censors initially balked at some of the promo spots; though the material had aired decades earlier, it was thought too provocative. About one thing, at least, Archie Bunker was spot on. "Those were the days..." —MATTHEW MCCANN FENTON

ALL IN THE FAMILY

JUST THE FACTS

ALL IN THE FAMILY

YEARS ON AIR
1971–83 (1979–83 as *Archie Bunker's Place*)

TOP NIELSEN CHARTING
1st for five straight seasons (from 1971–72 to 1975–76)

EMMYS WON
10; 3 consecutive Emmys for Outstanding Comedy Series

FIRST IMPRESSIONS
"Nothing less than an insult...too bad this bundle from Britain wasn't turned back at the shoreline." *–Daily Variety*

GROUNDBREAKING MOMENT First sitcom to feature the sound of a flushing toilet on TV.

ORIGINAL TITLE
Those Were the Days (pilot)

ORIGINAL CASTING
Mickey Rooney was considered for Archie but was dropped when he insisted Lear change the character to an elderly, blind Vietnam veteran who was an amateur detective; Penny Marshall for Gloria

SPIN-OFFS/SEQUELS
Maude, *The Jeffersons*, *Gloria*, *Good Times*, *Archie Bunker's Place*, *Checking In*, *704 Hauser*

WHAT DIDN'T MAKE IT ON THE AIR
Mike walking downstairs zipping his fly (implying he'd been having sex with Gloria); Archie yelling "Goddamn it!"

BEHIND THE SCENES
Reiner and Struthers dated in real life years before the series; he went on to marry the woman Struthers beat out for the Gloria role, Penny Marshall.

WHAT'S IN A NAME
Archie's original name was Archie Justice; his son-in-law, Mike Stivic, was originally Irish (rather than Polish) and was to be named Dickie.

WHAT DID THEY KNOW?
Labor leader George Meany denounced the show as an insult to the American working man; civil rights leader Whitney Young feared it would fan the fire of racial tensions.

CHEERS

THIS BEANTOWN ENSEMBLE RAISED THE BAR FOR EVERY OTHER SITCOM TO COME

NBC WAS THINKING CHEAP BEER—what it got was vintage champagne. All revved up over a series of popular Miller Lite commercials that featured famous athletes bellying up to the bar, the network went looking for a new sitcom with the same hell-raising atmosphere. While the writing team of Glen and Le Charles, coming off their success with *Taxi*, obliged with a com edy set in a Boston bar (modeled on that city's real Bull & Finch and revolving around a randy retired Red Sox pitcher, the tw *Fawlty Towers* fans decided to swing for the fences when it cam to scripts and casting. ✦ It's painful when TV writers boast tha they're going for Spencer Tracy-Katharine Hepburn-style repar tee and end up with dialogue more on the level of *Who's th Boss?* But with Sam Malone (Ted Danson) and Diane Chamber (Shelley Long), the art of the sitcom came damn close to 1940s era sparkle. The intercourse (verbal only—at least at the start between Sam, a likable lunkhead with a drinking problem in hi past, and Diane, a pretentious, just-slumming grad-student bar maid, was a cocktail of crackling wordplay and sexual tension

JUST THE FACTS

CHEERS

YEARS ON AIR
1982–93

TOP NIELSEN CHARTING
1st (1990–91 season); top 10 rating 8 of 11 seasons; it is also one of only two shows to have finished both first and last in the weekly ratings (*Lou Grant* is the other).

EMMYS WON
Won 28 out of a total of 117; Rhea Perlman won Outstanding Supporting Actress in a Comedy Series three consecutive years.

ORIGINAL CASTING
William Devane (*Knots Landing*) and Fred Dryer (*Hunter*) were early contenders for the role of Sam Malone. Robert Prosky (roll-call sergeant Stan Jablonsky on *Hill Street Blues*) was originally cast as Coach.

OCCUPATIONAL HAZARDS
George Wendt gained 75 pounds during the season, lost it during hiatus, then gained it back during the next season.

ON THE HOUSE
During filming, the cast drank a concoction called near beer, with salt added to provide a foamy head. It was widely detested.

SPIN-OFFS
Frasier

POSTPRODUCTION NOTES
When *Cheers* was over, Danson got the bar itself as a memento for his Malibu home.

4

Diane (walking into the bar and announcing portentously): "I have a chilling tale!" Sam: "Yeah, but it's cute and you wiggle it." ✦ In its secondary roles, *Cheers* had a further embarrassment of riches: John Ratzenberger as trivia-geek mama's-boy mailman Cliff ("Due to the shape of the North American elk's esophagus, even if it could speak, it could not pronounce the word *lasagna*"); George Wendt as cuddly but beleaguered bar-stool fixture Norm ("It's a dog-eat-dog world, and I'm wearing Milk-Bone underwear"); Rhea Perlman as caustic barmaid Carla (she refers to Diane as "stick," one of the more polite nicknames); as well as Kelsey Grammer as pompous shrink Frasier Crane, and Woody Harrelson as dim-bulb bartender Woody Boyd. ✦ By its fourth season, the James Burrows-directed show was such a ratings bonanza it was able to survive Long's departure; when Kirstie Alley stepped in as the sultry but insecure bar owner Rebecca Howe, *Cheers* didn't lose its fizz for an instant. One key to its longevity at the top of the Nielsen heap (it was a top five show for seven straight years) was the Charles-Burrows-Charles team's careful avoidance of easy sentimentality—to *Cheers*, the Very Special Episodes about "serious" topics that drag down many aging comedies were anathema. Its humor was adult, but never grown-up. ✦ When *Cheers* closed its doors in 1993 (because Danson wanted to move on and no one wanted to continue without him), the characters were spectacularly unredeemed. They had made it through 11 seasons with their frailties as firmly in place as when they first descended the steps to the bar "where everybody knows your name." And that's something worth drinking to. —MMF/PHOTOGRAPH BY TONY COSTA

THE WITTIEST, CREEPIEST SCI-FI SHOW OF ALL TIME? 'X'-ACTLY.

IT WAS WRITER AND EX-SURFER (*X*-surfer?) Chris Carter's notion to do a contemporary variation on one of the favorite shows of his youth, the 1974-75 supernatural series *Kolchak: The Night Stalker*. Except that where Darren McGavin's Kolchak was a neurotic loner vainly trying to convince everyone that bad juju exists all around us, it was Carter's first stroke of genius to give his neurotic loner, Fox Mulder (David Duchovny), a female partner, Dana Scully (Gillian Anderson), who would provide skepticism, collegial support, and a constant undercurrent of sexual tension. ✦ Together, working as FBI agents assigned to "X-Files"—unsolved cases involving inexplicable occurrences—Mulder and Scully uncovered not only lots of monsters (vampires, Frankensteinian creatures, nerds with the ability to shoot fatal jolts of electricity at their victims), but also—and this was Carter's second stroke of genius—a governmental plot of massive proportions. ✦ The result was far and away the best television sci-fi since *The Twilight Zone*, and in the consistency of its writing and depth of characterization, a show that is in many respects superior to Rod Serling's vaunted '60s anthology series. By its second season, *The X-Files* had spawned a cult large enough to give the fledgling Fox network a big boost in both ratings and respect—and to turn Duchovny and Anderson (as well as the dashingly handsome Carter) into TV idols the equal of any in the medium's history. But *The X-Files*

proved to be no flash in the media pan; there was none of *Twin Peaks*' great-first-season-and-let's-get-crazy implosion. ✦ Shot in Vancouver for its first five seasons (production moved to Los Angeles for the 1998-99 season), *The X-Files* has a uniquely dark, dank look to match the bleakness of its message, which flashes across the show's opening credits: "Trust no one." A conspiracy theorist's dream show, *The X-Files* assumes that the American government is not above colluding with aliens to keep an otherworldly invasion a secret from its citizens, and it is to Carter's credit that the show has managed to make that premise seem more credible than absurd. ✦ As the series proceeded, Mulder and Scully were surrounded by a supporting cast that came to include their protective boss, Walter Skinner (Mitch Pileggi), the foreboding Cigarette-Smoking Man (William B. Davis), the trio of oddball computer geniuses called the Lone Gunmen (Tom Braidwood, Dean Haglund, and Bruce Harwood), and Mulder's archenemy, the savage Agent Alex Krycek (Nicholas Lea). While none of these characters could be called rich in depth, they maintain the series' air of mystery and unexpectedness. Mulder and Scully are a different matter; they are as soulful and complicated a pair as any heroes television has offered up. —KEN TUCKER

5

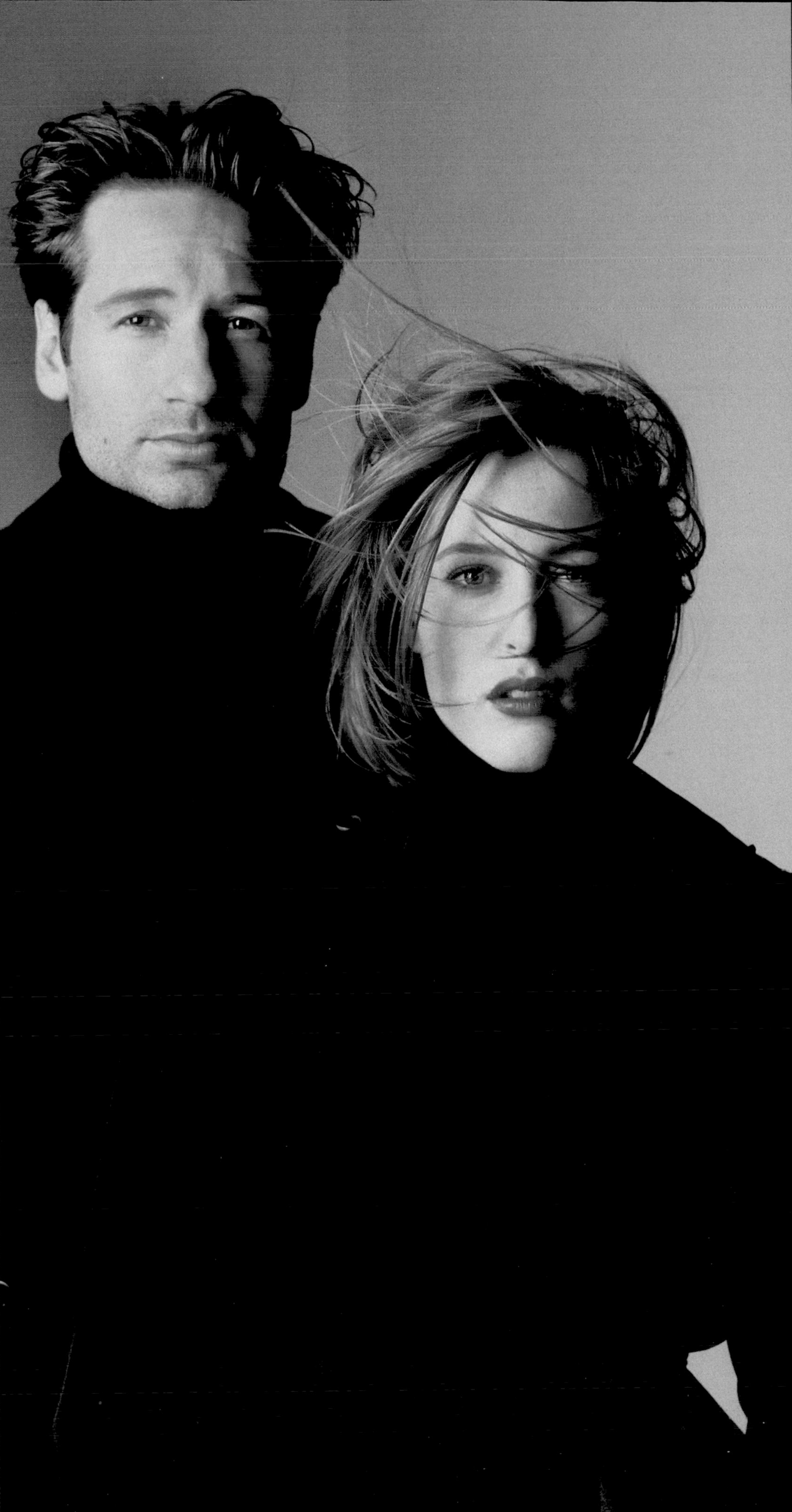

JUST THE FACTS

THE X-FILES

YEARS ON AIR 1993–present

TOP NIELSEN CHARTING 20th (1996–97)

EMMYS WON 9

ORIGINAL CASTING Anderson almost didn't get the role of Dana Scully; producers were aiming for a more "typically marketable beauty."

SLIGHTLY EMBARRASSING PREVIOUS CAREER HIGHLIGHTS Duchovny costarred with Veronica Hamel and Nancy McKeon in a 1992 TV movie called *Baby Snatcher.* Anderson was the voice of Lisa Kelly on the audiocassette edition of Anne Rice's S&M novel, *Exit to Eden.*

EARLY NONINFLUENCES Carter claims that he never watched *Star Trek* and wasn't a fan of sci-fi in general.

CROSSOVER DREAMS *The X-Files made* cliff-hanger/cash-cow history at the end of the 1997–98 season, when it left viewers who wanted to know how the plot was resolved with only one choice: to buy a movie ticket over that summer for the film version of *The X-Files.*

CROSSOVER HALLUCINATIONS Duchovny has been quoted as saying, "We're just as real as *NYPD Blue* or *ER.* Their subject matter is just a little tamer."

WHAT DID THEY KNOW? "Pity the poor critic who has to sit there with a big grin on his face and watch the whole stupid thing.... [*The*] *X-Files* is too iffy and inconclusive to be satisfying." –*The Washington Post,* Sept. 10, 1993

ART DOESN'T IMITATE LIFE Despite the leanings of their characters, Duchovny has admitted he doesn't believe in UFOs, while Anderson says she does.

JUST THE FACTS

I LOVE LUCY

YEARS ON AIR 1951–57

TOP NIELSEN CHARTING
No. 1 for four years; never ranked below 3rd

PRECOCIOUS YOUTH
After a young Lucille Ball spent one semester at a New York drama school, her mother received a telegram telling her Lucy just didn't have the talent to pursue acting.

INSPIRATION
The TV pilot was based on an earlier radio show starring Ball called *My Favorite Husband.*

FIRSTS
Lucy was the first sitcom to be seen in 10 million homes—at a time when there were only about 15 million TV sets in the U.S.

MAKING HISTORY
More than twice as many people (about 44 million of 'em) saw the Jan. 19, 1953, episode in which Little Ricky was born than watched President Eisenhower's inauguration the following day.

LIFE IMITATES ART
Lucy's real-life baby (Desi Arnaz IV) was delivered by Caesarean section on the night that episode aired.

ORIGINAL CASTING
Lucy reportedly wanted Gale Gordon (later Mr. Mooney on *The Lucy Show*) and Bea Benaderet (later the mom on *Petticoat Junction*) to play Fred and Ethel Mertz.

LUCY IS READY FOR HER CLOSE-UP NOW
Shooting on *I Love Lucy* was supervised by cinematographer Karl Freund, who'd earned his reputation by working with Greta Garbo. *Lucy* was the first TV show shot on 35 mm film, like a movie.

CAMEOS
Everyone from Bob Hope to William Holden, Harpo Marx, Rock Hudson, John Wayne, and Orson Welles

SEMPER FI
Arnaz and Ball allegedly stipulated in their original deal with CBS that their characters couldn't flirt with anyone else. Rules aside, the couple split, divorcing in 1960.

SPIN-OFFS
The Lucy-Desi Comedy Hour. Ball went on to star in *The Lucy Show, Here's Lucy,* and *Life With Lucy.*

THE RUBBER-FACED REDHEAD'S COMIC BALLETS WERE TUTU FUNNY FOR WORDS

I LOVE LUCY

A LACKLUSTER CAREER in the movies had earned her the snarky nickname Queen of the Bs. But when Lucille Ball turned to TV, she ruled supreme. A half hour of madcap schemes and bilingual squabbling, *I Love Lucy* became TV's first bona fide hit sitcom, pulling in better ratings than the coronation of a real-life queen named Elizabeth. ✦ And more than four decades after its 1951 debut, the sun hasn't set on Lucy's empire. Thanks to endless reruns, even casual couch potatoes know the dizzy redhead's slapstick ballets: Lucy failing to keep up with the conveyor belt at the chocolate factory, stomping grapes at a winery, slurring her way through a Vitameatavegamin commercial. Intoxicating stuff. ✦ But America almost never got to love *Lucy* at all. In the late '40s, CBS approached Ball—then starring in a radio comedy—about a TV series. Hoping to shore up a shaky marriage, Ball insisted her husband, Desi Arnaz, costar. A Latino leading man? A mixed marriage in prime time? Conservative CBS said *muchas gracias*, but no. Only after Lucy and Desi toured a hit vaudeville version of the show did the network reluctantly buckle. ✦ *Lucy* made other innovations, too. The show was the first to be filmed in front of a live studio audience, the first to use the now-standard three-camera setup, the first where the stars owned syndication rights (snagging Ball and Arnaz millions of dollars). ✦ And then there was Lucy herself: Though in some ways she was a typical '50s TV housewife—she cooked, cleaned, and tucked her hair under a kerchief—the show's running conceit was that Lucy was ambitious for a showbiz career all her own. How many times did she try to sneak on stage at Ricky's Tropicana club (and then have to 'splain herself later to Ricky)? Lucy may have been dizzy, but a dummy she was not. Indeed, one of the stipulations in Arnaz and Ball's original deal with CBS was that the show's humor could never hold anyone up to ridicule. ✦ Of course, there were limits to how far *Lucy* could push the envelope. When Ball's real-life pregnancy was written into the show, a hand-wringing CBS had a priest, a rabbi, and a Protestant minister on the set (the word *pregnant* was never used). The result of that condition was Little Ricky, whose 1953 birth hooked an amazing 72 percent of viewers. And the audiences kept watching until *Lucy* left the air four years later, still ranked No. 1 (a feat matched only by *Andy Griffith* and *Seinfeld*). Almost a half century later, Lucy's zany antics are still running—and rerunning and rerunning (so much so that it's been estimated her face has been seen by more people than anybody else's—ever). A showbiz career? It looks like Lucy got her wish.

—MMF/PHOTOGRAPH BY LOOMIS DEAN

6

JUST THE FACTS

LARRY SANDERS SHOW

YEARS ON AIR
1992–98

TOP NIELSEN CHARTING
Not available because it was a cable show.

EMMYS WON
The show garnered several dozen nominations in a number of categories and lost every time but one. (Rip Torn's Emmy win for the '95 season made him the only *Larry Sanders* nominee ever to take home a trophy.)

LIFE IMITATES ART
After one critically acclaimed season, NBC offered Shandling a four-year, $20 million deal to take over David Letterman's old spot when that comic bolted for CBS.

DID ART IMITATE LIFE?
In 1994, Shandling explained the difference between his character and himself by saying, "He's 43; I'm 44."

CASTING CALL
John Glover auditioned as Artie but was a runner-up for the role.

HUMBLE BEGINNINGS
Shandling got his start writing for sitcoms such as *Sanford and Son* and *Welcome Back, Kotter.*

PRODUCTION NOTES
The "show" sequences were shot on video to simulate the bright, glossy feel of an actual talk show; the backstage sequences were shot on film to achieve a murky, grainy texture.

THE LARRY SANDERS SHOW

HEY NOW! HERE WAS SHOWBIZ AT ITS UNEXPURGATED BEST.

THESE WERE THE FINAL WORDS heard on *Th Larry Sanders Show*: "I'm such a prick." Spoken by the usual obsequious sidekick Hank Kingsley (Jeffrey Tambor), it was h apology for blowing up after Larry (Garry Shandling) cut sho Hank's farewell speech on the talk show's final telecast. Th words were a perfect epitaph for *Sanders*, which wallowed br liantly in the self-loathing world of Hollywood. ✦ But thes aren't words you'd hear on a commercial network. Because aired on HBO, Shandling's satire of late-night shows was fre from censorship and ratings constraints. As Shandlin explained in 1994: "We can show people in the show-busines world talking as they really do, which does include profanit Also, we explore a dark side of people's personalities that ofte network shows aren't willing to explore, because it's not alwa

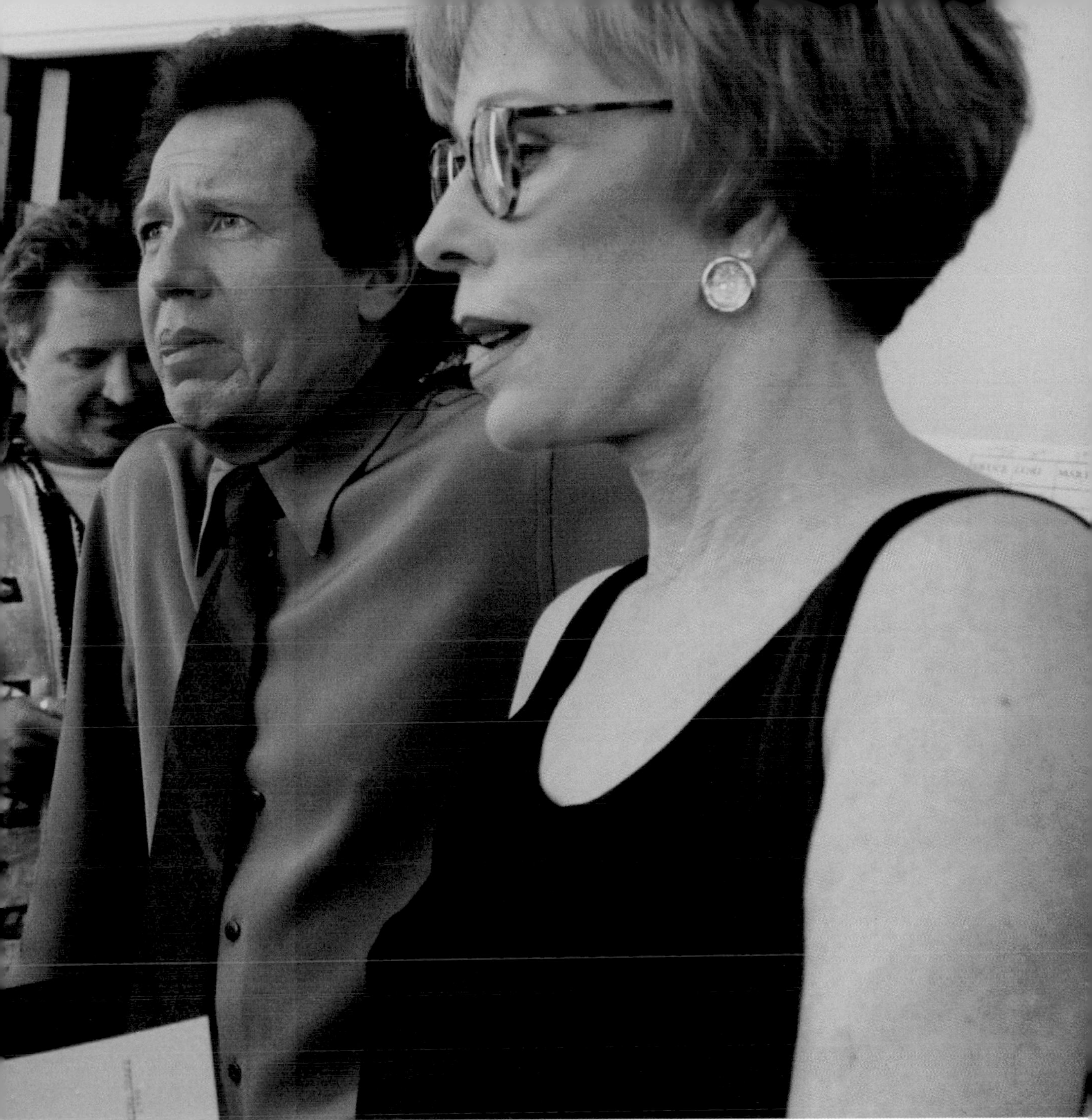

easant." ✦ Maybe not, but it was always funny; we even ughed as we squirmed. Consider this exchange between rry and Jerry (Jeremy Piven), an ex-writer, backstage before e last show. ✦ JERRY: "I just wanted to see, after you fired e and f---ed up my life, if you'd stand there and smile at me e we were old buddies." ✦ LARRY (smiling like they were old ddies): "Well, now you know." ✦ Shandling wasn't the only lebrity who skewered himself on *Sanders*. Such stars as rry Seinfeld, Roseanne, Warren Beatty, and Sharon Stone ed up for the opportunity. Larry became convinced that vid Duchovny had a crush on him. Ellen DeGeneres slept with rry. And Carol Burnett whispered the immortal words "I saw ur balls" after Larry's loincloth slipped during a Tarzan etch. ✦ Although its scripts remained rooted in the latest late-night news (David Letterman's defection to CBS, Jay Leno's ascension), *Sanders* is guaranteed to stand the test of time thanks to its incisive portrayal of the behind-the-scenes politics of showbiz. There's the blustery boss, Artie (Rip Torn), whose power lies in knowing when to kick ass—and when to kiss it; the cynical writer, Phil (Wallace Langham), whose creativity can be fueled only by his own personal misery; and Larry's assistant, Beverly (Penny Johnson), who seems unassuming but secretly knows all. ✦ And then there's Larry, the passive-aggressive star who just wants everyone to love him. Long after its catchphrases (Larry's "No flipping," Hank's "Hey now!") have been forgotten, *Sanders* will be remembered as the most brutally honest and hilarious portrait of Hollywood in television history. —BRUCE FRETTS/PHOTOGRAPH BY GAIL ALBERT HALABAN

JUST THE FACTS

HILL STREET BLUES

YEARS ON AIR
1981–87

TOP NIELSEN CHARTING
27th (1982–83)

EMMYS WON
Total of 18, including a record eight for its first season. In 1982, all of the nominees for Outstanding Supporting Actor in a Drama Series were from *Hill Street Blues*; Michael Conrad won.

ORIGINAL TITLE
The pilot was a 1981 NBC TV movie called *Hill Street Station*. NBC wanted something catchier for the series, and considered a number of names, including *The Blue Zoo*. Finally, the producers compromised with *Hill Street Blues*.

CASTING NOTES
Before joining the cast as Lieutenant Buntz in 1985, Dennis Franz appeared in several episodes of *Hill Street* as the sadistically depraved Det. Sal Benedetto.

PRESCIENT CASTING
Ken Olin, who would later find fame on *thirtysomething*, had a supporting role as Det. Harry Garibaldi during *Hill Street*'s 1984–85 season. David Caruso, who got white-hot on *NYPD Blue*, appeared as an Irish gang leader early in its run.

LITERARY CAMEO
Such was the prestige of *Hill Street Blues* that playwright David Mamet agreed to write an episode during the last season.

ART IMITATES LIFE
Charles Haid (Officer Renko) was the real-life husband of Debi Richter, who played Renko's trashy wife; Barbara Bosson was the real-life wife of the top banana on *Hill Street* (no, not Capt. Furillo; producer Steven Bochco).

WHO BROUGHT THE BLUES TO HILL STREET?
Composer Mike Post wrote the beautiful jazz piano score that became the show's signature. It appeared briefly on the pop charts in 1981.

HILL STREET BLUES

ITS TELE-VÉRITÉ STYLE MADE COPS SUDDENLY SEEM HUMAN

'HILL STREET BLUES' TOOK THE COP SHOW AND TURNED IT upside down. Law-enforcement officials had previously been portrayed on TV as either dutiful civil servants (*Dragnet, Adam-12*) or larger-than-life superheroes (*The Untouchables, Starsky & Hutch*). *Hill Street* took a more humanistic view, painting cops as complicated individuals (and paving the way for such tele-vérité fare as *Law & Order, Homicide: Life on the Street,* and cocreator Steven Bochco's own *NYPD Blue*). ✦ Foremost among these was soft-spoken, intense Capt. Frank Furillo (Daniel J. Travanti), the supervisor of a chaotic precinct in an unnamed city (the series was initially set in the Bronx, but NBC deleted all mentions of New York City to make the show seem more universal). Furillo oversaw a bustling squad room, but he spent much of his time dealing with his hectoring ex-wife, Fay (Barbara Bosson), and carrying on a torrid relationship with sultry, bleeding-heart public defender Joyce Davenport (Veronica Hamel), who would later become his wife in the series. ✦ Each installment opened with a roll call that set up that week's stories. These briefings were initially delivered by Sgt. Phil Esterhaus (Michael Conrad), a gentle soul who turned out the troops with his trademark phrase, "Let's be careful out there." After Conrad died in 1984, Esterhaus suffered a fatal heart attack while making love to his flamboyant girlfriend, Grace Gardner (Barbara Babcock). He was replaced by Stan "Stosh" Jablonski (Robert Prosky), whose less-refined manner was summed up by his blunt tag line, "Let's do it to them before they do it to us." ✦ *Hill Street*'s teeming ensemble swelled to 17 at one point, but several characters stood out: good ol' boy Andrew Renko (Charles Haid) and his profoundly decent partner, Bobby Hill (Michael Warren), who was the show's conscience; Betty Thomas' Lucy Bates, the most believable TV policewoman ever; gung ho Emergency Action Team leader Lieut. Howard Hunter (James B. Sikking); and growling undercover detective Mick "Mad Dog" Belker (Bruce Weitz), who often provided the gallows humor. ✦ Comedy and tragedy frequently collided, as in the episode in which self-appointed superhero Captain Freedom (Dennis Dugan) was shot and killed by a thug. As he expired, Belker barked at him, "You die, you hair bag, I'll kick your butt across the block!" (Belker's other terms of endearment included "Dog breath," "Toe jam," and "Maggot mouth.") ✦ As the squad investigated cases ranging from domestic abuse to gangland warfare, the series examined important social issues while avoiding preachiness. Like a great blues song, *Hill Street* featured recurring themes, a soulful tone, and a sense of joy underlying the melancholia. These cops had it bad, and that was good. —BF

8

DECADES BEFORE VIAGRA, THIS WAS AMERICA'S MAGIC LATE-NIGHT BEDTIME PILL

THE TONIGHT SHOW

9

FOR MILLIONS OF AMERICANS, it was a comforting, consistent, comedic lullaby. Every night for three decades, they'd drift off to sleep as a twinkle-eyed, silver-haired Nebraskan swung an invisible golf club, made some alimony jokes, and inspired throaty ho-ho-hos from his eager sidekick. ✦ Never again will anyone rule late-night TV as did Johnny Carson. Over the course of some 4,500 shows, he turned *The Tonight Show* into a pre-sleep ritual, launched a thousand stand-up careers, and reached the kind of fame where last names are unnecessary: "Heeeeere's Johnny!" was enough. ✦ Of course, there *was* life before Carson. *Tonight* debuted in 1954 with Steve Allen, a former radio announcer and pianist, as its host. "Steverino" was brilliantly experimental. Years before David Letterman, he liked to set up a mike on the street and banter with anyone who walked by. (Once, on *The Steve Allen Show*, the host covered himself in tea bags and took a dip in hot water.) ✦ When Allen signed off after three years, former game-show host Jack Paar took over. Paar made for riveting TV: Not only did he conduct razor-sharp interviews with the likes of Fidel Castro and Robert F. Kennedy, but he was prone to on-air meltdowns, crying when guests said something moving. And when NBC censored a joke about a water closet, he walked off the set, saying, "There must be a better way to make a living than this." A month later, Paar returned, starting the show with the words "As I was saying before I was interrupted..." ✦ After Paar walked away for good, NBC turned to Carson, host of a popular (ungrammatically titled) game show called *Who Do You Trust?* On Oct. 1, 1962, Carson was introduced by Groucho Marx; when he was greeted by applause, Carson responded, "Boy, you'd think it was Vice President Nixon." In contrast to Paar, Carson was a cool ironist with Jack Benny's sense of timing and a bent for double entendres. His monologues were masterful when they worked—and just as funny when they didn't ("Did they clear the hall?" he'd ask). Carson kept the guest segments as light as a soufflé. We watched tarantulas from the San Diego Zoo crawl up his arm and Bette Midler crawl on his desk to serenade him. There was nary a tear, except maybe when viewers watched Tiny Tim's 1969 marriage. ✦ By the late '80s, Carson was still late-night king, but cable had started to erode network viewership, and life at NBC was getting less and less fun; by 1991, he had had enough and casually announced his retirement. The next year, Jay Leno assumed the reins at *Tonight*—and a juicy, headline-grabbing battle of talk hosts ensued. The passive-aggressive David Letterman (who had lost out as Carson's successor) won the initial ratings skirmishes, but then Leno and his barb-free humor put *Tonight* back on top, where it remains. As Allen said on that very first night, "I want to give you the bad news first. This show is going to go on forever."

—MMF/PHOTOGRAPH BY ARTHUR SCHATZ

JUST THE FACTS

THE TONIGHT SHOW

YEARS ON AIR
1954–present

TOP NIELSEN CHARTING
Not available

EMMYS WON 9

FAITHFUL VIEWERS
More than 50 million watched Carson's last show on May 22, 1992; the second-highest rated show was aired on Dec. 17, 1969, featuring the marriage of Tiny Tim to Miss Vicki.

BATHROOM HUMOR
A casual joke by Carson in 1973 about a pending toilet-paper shortage caused a run on bathroom tissue at supermarkets nationwide.

DOING WELL
In 1978, at the peak of Carson's popularity, *The Tonight Show* snared almost 4 out of every 10 late-night viewers. By 1992, the show was earning an estimated $100 million per year.

GETTING RICH
In 1980, Carson Productions took over *The Tonight Show*, netting a $50 million annual licensing fee; Carson himself reportedly received $20 million of this amount. The ownership of the show reverted to NBC after Carson's exodus.

BRANCHING OUT
Carson Productions also supplied *Late Night With David Letterman* and the sitcom *Amen* to NBC, and produced the hit movie *The Big Chill*.

OOPS!
In his first outing as the new host of *The Tonight Show*, Leno deliberately failed to mention his predecessor, Carson. Leno later called it "the biggest mistake of my entire life."

JUST THE
FACTS

THE SIMPSONS

YEARS ON AIR
1989–present

TOP NIELSEN CHARTING
30th (1989–90, 1992–93)

EMMYS WON 12; six cast members won Outstanding Voice-Over in 1992

HOW IT ALL BEGAN
Matt Groening created the *Simpsons* characters when he was in high school as part of a never-published novel called *Mean Kids*, which he described as "my version of *Catcher in the Rye*."

WHAT'S IN A NAME?
Bart is an anagram for *brat*.

WAITING FOR HIS VOICE TO CHANGE
The part of Bart is actually voiced by a woman, Nancy Cartwright.

OTHER VOICES, OTHER ROOMS
The Simpsons has been the greatest magnet for big-star cameos since *Batman*. Guest voices have included Elizabeth Taylor, Michael Jackson, Dustin Hoffman, Johnny Carson, Jackie Mason, Glenn Close, Penny Marshall, Paul McCartney, George Harrison, Ringo Starr, Darryl Strawberry, Tony Bennett, Larry King, and Danny DeVito.

ART IMITATES LIFE
Groening's real family were named Homer (dad), Margaret (mom), and Lisa and Maggie (sisters). Still, he insists the show is not autobiographical.

ANOTHER ALL-AMERICAN PRODUCT MADE WITH FOREIGN LABOR
More than 100 animators (mostly in South Korea) labor for six months at a time to produce each episode of *The Simpsons*.

10

IN THE MID-'80S, MATT GROENING, INDIGENT LOS ANGELES-BASED newspaper cartoonist, was approached by a fan, producer-director James L. Brooks, to provide some animated cartoons to run between sketches on *The Tracey Ullman Show*. Groening came up with the Simpsons, bright-yellow-skinned dysfunctionals who debuted in April 1987. Dad: Homer—stupid but wily, loving but greedy, with an insatiable appetite for doughnuts in the morning and beer at night. Mom: Marge—wise and kind, possessor of a thick column of blue hair. Son: Bart—the consummate 10-year-old wise guy. Daughter: Lisa—the consummate 8-year-old "sensitive child." Baby: Maggie—no known characteristics except for an addiction to her pacifier. ✦ The Fox network gave the Simpson clan its own show in 1989 (soon after *Ullman* was off the air), and the results proved spectacular: Quickly, the show became the wittiest cartoon ever made for TV, teeming with memorable characters populating the town of Springfield, extending far beyond the vivid, squabbling, affectionate family at its center. Miraculously, the series survived its first few years as an international pop-cult phenomenon, characterized by much solemn media hand-wringing over Bart's guilt-free impudence and his rude catchphrase, "Don't have a cow, man!" *The Simpsons* went on to become a deep, rich show—one that, as Groening has not-at-all-immodestly said, "rewards you for paying attention," not least of all because many of its jokes and plots supply an incisive, hilarious critique of the media that both celebrates and pillories it. Homer, watching *60 Minutes*, sighs contentedly, "Television—teacher, mother, secret lover!" getting closer to the heart of the medium's appeal than entire generations of pop-culture scholars. ✦ The Simpsons have confronted everything from alcoholism (Homer's hangout, Moe's Tavern, is a den of substance abuse presided over by the belching Barney; no show has made drinking seem less appealing) to religion (nerdy next-door neighbor Ned Flanders is an unquestioning fundamentalist given to pronouncements like "I say there are some things we don't want to know—important things!"). If Groening's politics come across as liberal-libertarian, the show is ultimately a deeply moral one. The core cast of actors providing the voices for the Simpsons and beyond—Dan Castellaneta, Julie Kavner, Yeardley Smith, Nancy Cartwright, Hank Azaria, and all-time utility player Harry Shearer—have helped give the series an emotional resonance found on only the finest television series. —KT

THE SIMPSONS

WITH THIS WITTY, CYNICAL 'TOON, FLEDGLING FOX HIT A HOMER RUN

BANG-ZOOM! KRAMDEN AND CO.'S ANTICS TOOK US TO THE MOON!

"THE FIRST ONE WAS ABOUT FOUR, FIVE MINUTES," recalled writer Walter Stone. "He comes home from work, she's steaming. She says 'Go to the store,' or something. Just five minutes of that." From one humble off-the-cuff running sketch in 1951 on *Cavalcade of Stars*, which featured Jackie Gleason as the MC, grew a TV comedy whose proportions were even more epic than its star's. *The Honeymooners* represented a number of historical firsts—it was the first spin-off series, the first show to present an unvarnished picture of blue-collar life—but the reason it endures is that its characters and their relationships were timeless right off the bat. ✦ In a landscape in which Ozzie and Harriet Nelson were the norm, Ralph and Alice Kramden were real. Between "Bang-zoom!" and "Baby, you're the greatest!" they caught the arc of marriage and magnified it until the only recourse was laughter. Gleason submerged his charismatic bluster into this little big man: Brooklynite bus driver Ralph is a study in the comic frustrations of the working stiff, ballooning with dreams (furniture shampoo, Kram-Nor's hair restorer, glow-in-the-dark shoe polish), sagging when reality hits, then shrugging and moving on. Audrey Meadows played Alice as the Good Shrew, just as ready with the fat jokes ("If you knew how to throw your weight around, you wouldn't leave it where it is") as with exasperated understanding. And then there was Ed Norton: sewer worker, coconspirator, best friend, patsy. Art Carney pulled off the impossible trick of seeming both smarter and denser than his costar; in essence, he was the Sancho Panza of 358 Chauncey Street. *Cavalcade* cowriter Coleman Jacoby said it was "Carney who gave [the show] a note of originality and who took the edge off the brutal aspect of it." ✦ It's startling to realize that *The Honeymooners* series wasn't truly a hit the first time around. Sure, audiences loved the recurring sketches, first on the DuMont Network's *Cavalcade* (where Pert Kelton played the original Alice) and then on CBS' 1952–55 *The Jackie Gleason Show*. But in 1955, when Gleason signed a $6 million two-season contract to spin *Honeymooners* off on its own, the deal was to last only a year thanks to unexpected competition from *The Perry Como Show* on NBC. When *The Honeymooners* finished 20th in the ratings, Gleason called it quits and sold the 39 videotaped episodes to CBS, which later sold them into syndication. There "the classic 39" ran and reran and reran, until they became almost biblical in their towering impact. Okay, so they don't do the Hucklebuck in the Bible—but what Gleason and Co. wrought still stands as sitcom gospel. —TY BURR

THE HONEYMOONERS

JUST THE FACTS

THE HONEYMOONERS

YEARS ON AIR AS AN INDEPENDENT SERIES 1955–56

TOP NIELSEN CHARTING 20th

DRIVE, THEY SAID
Though *Cavalcade*'s writing staff reportedly considered making Ralph Kramden a cop, they settled on a bus driver because there was more opportunity for him to get annoyed.

CASH COW
Buick offered Gleason $6 million to turn the sketches from *The Jackie Gleason Show* into its own series.

STROKE OF GENIUS
The show was broadcast live, but Gleason insisted it also be preserved on high-quality film so he could sell it in reruns.

PRODUCTION NOTES
Gleason, whose idea of rehearsing was to read through the script once before going on live television, had a standard distress signal for when he forgot his lines: He would pat his stomach. This would cue the others to begin improvising.

IGNOMINIOUS END
Gleason revived the *Honeymooners* characters in 1966 as part of an hour-long variety program, *The Jackie Gleason Show*, with the Kramdens and Nortons performing musical numbers.

LOST AND FOUND
In 1985, Gleason "discovered" old episodes of *The Honeymooners* that had aired as sketches on *The Jackie Gleason Show*; these were edited into 30-minute packages and eventually entered rerun heaven alongside the classic 39.

M*A*S*H

WAR WAS HELL—AND HELLISHLY FUNNY

THE AUTHOR OF THE ORIGINAL NOVEL HATED IT. The director of the earlier film, Robert Altman, called it "terrible." In its first season, even the public didn't like it too much. But over 11 seasons and 251 episodes, the TV version of *M*A*S*H* came to be regarded as one of the finest shows of all time. ✦ Before *M*A*S*H*, comedies about the military relied on farce—think *Hogan's Heroes* or *F Troop*. But from the show's 1972 debut, the goings-on at the 4,077th Mobile Army Surgical Hospital cut much deeper. Creator Larry Gelbart set out to establish a ground-breaking "dramedy" approach—to convey war's hilarity, heartbreak, and hellishness, all in the same episode. But it wasn't just the tone that was innovative; it was the technique, too. *M*A*S*H* was shot on film, and the camera moved cinematically, jumping from subplot to subplot to emphasize the ensemble. As the show developed, that inescapable sitcom fixture, the laugh track, was left out of the oper-

JUST THE FACTS

M*A*S*H

YEARS ON AIR 1972–83

TOP NIELSEN CHARTING 3rd (1982–83); finale garnered the highest rating share ever with 77 percent of households (125 million viewers).

EMMYS WON 14

BATTLE SCARS First antiwar sitcom (it was almost four times the length of real Korean War). Jamie Farr was the only actor who'd actually served in Korea.

ORIGINAL CASTING Alda didn't want the part of Hawkeye and signed on only eight hours before the first rehearsal. Stevenson actually wanted to portray Hawkeye himself.

ORIGINAL CONCEPT Based on a book by Richard Hornberger, a Korean War doctor

ALDA'S SALARY $10,000 for the pilot episode; by the final season, more than $5 million a year

HAWKEYE'S SALARY $413.50 a month

WHERE THAT SIGNPOST POINTS TO Coney Island, Burbank, San Francisco, Death Valley, Indianapolis, Decatur, Tokyo, Boston, and Seoul

SPIN-OFFS/SEQUELS *Trapper John, M.D.*; *AfterMASH*

AD RATES FOR FINALE $900,000 per minute

12

ating room, often the place where the doctors cracked wisest. Certain episodes even toyed with the boundaries of the genre: a black-and-white "documentary"; a first-person story in which the camera took the place of a wounded soldier. ✦ But what really made *M*A*S*H* enduring was the most basic asset of all: a crew of great characters. Bemused Henry Blake. Mischievous Trapper McIntire (and later, B.J. Hunnicutt). Perpetually outraged Margaret Houlihan. Intransigent Frank Burns. Humble yet capable Radar O'Reilly. And, of course, the wounded jester at the center of it all, Hawkeye Pierce. They changed and deepened over time: Margaret softened up, Hawkeye straightened up, Radar grew up. Even as actors left the series, our affection for the outfit abided: When the show's writers had the discharged Henry (McLean Stevenson) get shot down over the Sea of Japan, the public was outraged. ✦ More and more, star Alan Alda became the maestro of *M*A*S*H*, writing or directing a number of episodes. (He would go on to win Emmys for acting, writing, *and* directing.) The show took on the flavor of his progressive political views and, some critics said, lost its edge. No matter. When the finale aired on Feb. 28, 1983, some 125 million people watched, echoing the sentiments expressed in the episode's title, "Goodbye, Farewell, and Amen," and adding one more: Thank you.

—CAREN WEINER/PHOTOGRAPH BY BILL EPPRIDGE

13

STAR TREK

ADMIT IT: WE'RE ALL SPACE CASES FOR THESE EARLY STAR WARRIORS

THE WORLD IS MADE UP OF TWO KINDS OF PEOPLE: the Faithful, those who embrace the *Star Trek* universe—the original series, the eight movies (a ninth is in production), the three spin-offs, even the "Beam me up, Scottie" greeting cards. And the Disbelievers, who sneer that William Shatner nailed it perfectly in a *Saturday Night Live* skit when he ordered a roomful of nerdy Trekkies to "get a life." ✦ Shatner's quip stung, and here's why: *Star Trek* fans do indeed hanker after a different life, but not necessarily the one belonging to Capt. James T. Kirk, the hammiest he-man of the 23rd century. No, what's kept us hooked on the show ever since its 1966 debut is nothing less than *Star Trek*'s optimistic vision of the future of humanity. In the World According to Trek, we're not destined to blow ourselves to smithereens or degenerate into *Blade Runner*-ish squalor. Instead, we'll spend our lives going "boldly where no man has gone before," unsullied by racism and sexism and untroubled by finances (no bank accounts, no ATMs). Who *wouldn't* want to go? ✦ As any fan could tell you, this utopia was conjured up by producer Gene Roddenberry, who pitched his concept as a "*Wagon Train* to the stars." Roddenberry's *real* plan was to tackle 1960s troubles—war, prejudice, the generation gap—in futuristic settings, using as the show's ruling triumvirate Kirk and his two top aides: the icy half-Vulcan Mr. Spock (Leonard Nimoy) and the cantankerous "He's dead, Jim" ship's doctor, "Bones" McCoy (DeForest Kelley). ✦ In its original run, *Trek* never made it into the top 25 of any season, and NBC pulled the plug in 1969. Yet 10 years later, like Tribbles that wouldn't stop breeding, reruns had popped up on more than 140 stations. In response, the original cast was reassembled in feature films, and a new series, *Star Trek: The Next Generation*, starring the charismatic British actor Patrick Stewart, went on in 1987. ✦ Of course, no salute to *Trek* is complete without fond acknowledgment of its raging cheese factor: the women's groin-level miniskirts, Kirk's interstellar libido, the distant planets that bore an eerie resemblance to an L.A. hillside. It's the show's corny edges that the Disbelievers often wince at: Why, they carp, won't this franchise die? ✦ Because, in an era of skyscraper-high monsters, *Star Trek* has always possessed something rare in pop culture—a real vision. And that trumps soulless state-of-the-art special effects any day of the week. —NANCY BILYEAU

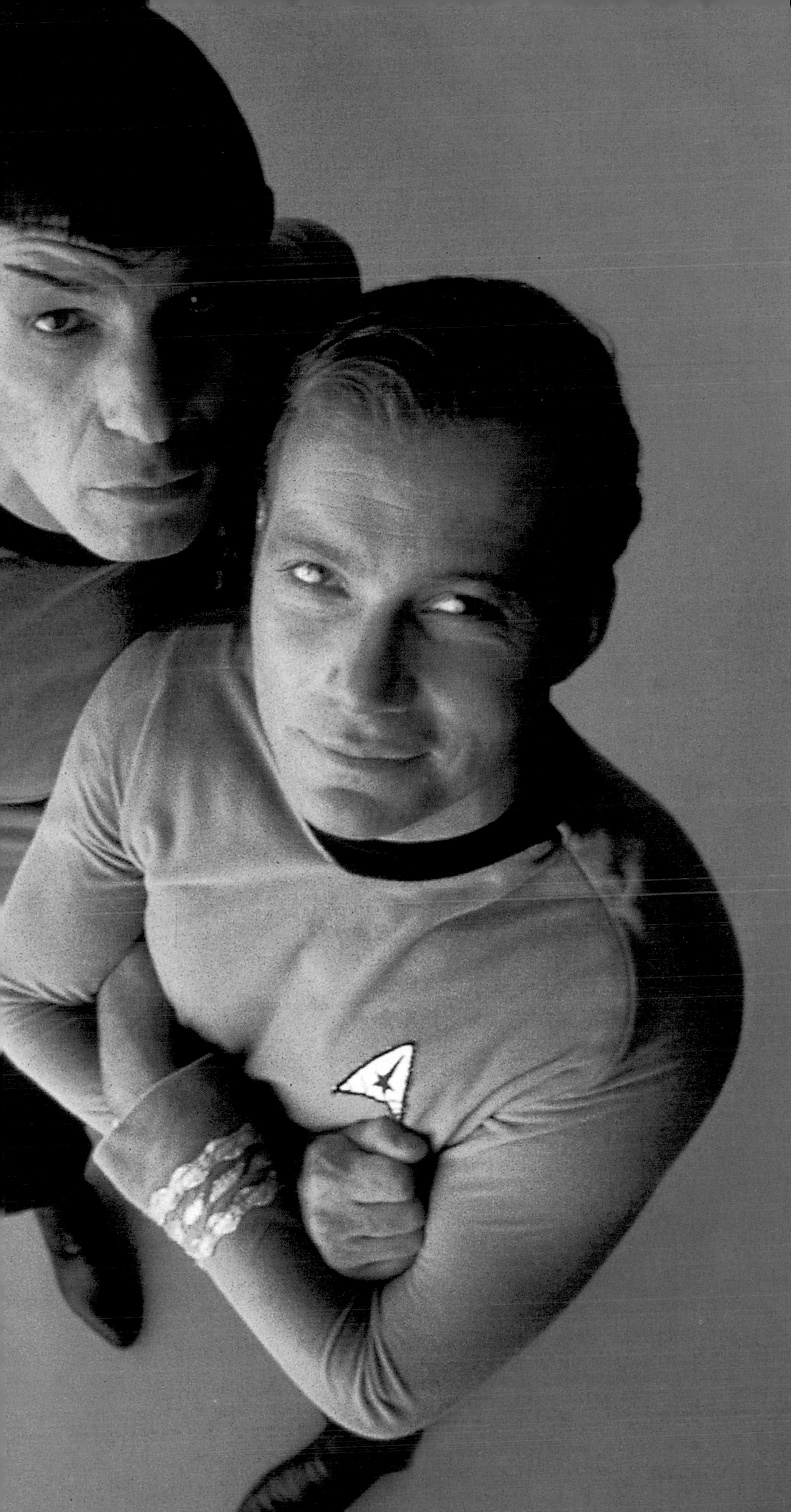

JUST THE FACTS

STAR TREK

YEARS ON AIR 1966–69

TOP NIELSEN CHARTING 52nd (1966–67)

EMMYS WON 0

ORIGINAL TITLE Though the first pilot was called *Star Trek*, a second pilot was made titled *Where No Man Has Gone Before*.

REPLACEMENT PARTS William Shatner replaced Jeffrey (*King of Kings*) Hunter from the pilot; Pavel Chekov (Walter Koenig) was added to give the show a youth boost, though supposedly the show's spin doctors insisted that he was hired because the Russian newspaper *Pravda* complained that an international space station was incomplete without a Russian aboard.

SPIN-OFFS/SEQUELS *Star Trek: The Next Generation; Voyager; Deep Space Nine*

SEMI-GROUNDBREAKING MOMENT *Star Trek* was credited with the first interracial kiss on network television when Kirk laid one on Lieutenant Uhura (Nichelle Nichols); however, according to Shatner, they never touched lips.

APOGEE OF WEIRDNESS Fans have created a vocabulary and grammar for the Klingon language, which has been taught as a university course.

ORIGINAL CASTING Both Lloyd Bridges and Jack Lord were offered the role of Captain Kirk before Shatner. Martin Landau was offered Spock's part but didn't think the proposition very logical.

CHEAPO PROPS Some of Dr. McCoy's high-tech medical instruments are actually salt and pepper shakers.

OY, IT'S AMOK TIME AGAIN Spock's V-fingered Vulcan felicitation, "Live Long and Prosper," is actually a traditional rabbinic blessing.

SEXUAL POLITICS IN THE 23RD CENTURY In the original pilot, a woman (Majel Barrett) was the second-in-command of the *Enterprise*. NBC couldn't live with this, however, and pressured Roddenberry to make Spock the first officer. Barrett was recast as Nurse Christine Chapel—and later married Roddenberry.

JUST THE FACTS

THE ED SULLIVAN SHOW

YEARS ON AIR 1948–71

TOP NIELSEN CHARTING 2nd (1956–57)

EMMYS WON 2

FOR THE RECORD BOOKS Longest-running variety show in history, second to *60 Minutes* for overall longevity.

ORIGINAL TITLE *You're the Top*

PROUD MOMENT Sullivan integrated prime time by regularly featuring African Americans as headliners and even embraced Pearl Bailey despite objections from the show's sponsors.

NOT-SO-PROUD MOMENT Caved in to advertiser pressure by denouncing performers alleged to have Communist sympathies.

PAYING THE TALENT Jerry Lewis and Dean Martin made their TV debut on the very first *Toast of the Town*. They split a fee of $200, which took up most of the talent budget that week ($375).

OTHER FIRSTS Acts that made their first U.S. TV appearances on *Sullivan* include the Beatles, Bob Hope, Lena Horne, Dinah Shore, Eddie Fisher, and Walt Disney.

PROTECTING THE SENSIBILITIES OF RIGHT-WING CRAZIES Bob Dylan was invited to appear on *Sullivan* in May 1963, but CBS told him he couldn't sing his satiric "Talking John Birch Society Blues." Dylan passed.

HE HAD A MEAN STREAK Reportedly columnist Harriet Van Horne wrote of Sullivan, "He got where he is not by having a personality, but by having no personality; he is the commonest common denominator." Sullivan sent her a short note back reading: "Dear Miss Van Horne, You bitch. Sincerely, Ed Sullivan."

BUT HE ALSO HAD A HEART Sullivan paid out of his own pocket for the funeral of the dancer Bill "Bojangles" Robinson, who died penniless. It was one of many acts of quiet personal generosity for which Sullivan was known among his friends.

ELVIS, THE BEATLES, LIZA, TOPO GIGIO—FOR A QUARTER CENTURY, IT WAS A "RILLY BIG SHEW"

THE ED SULLIVAN SHOW

14

OF ED SULLIVAN'S STIFF, FINGER-POINTING STYLE of bringing on his guests, radio comic Fred Allen once said, "A dog could do that, if you rubbed meat on the actors." His introductions were famously inept ("Here's José Feliciano. He's blind, and he's Puerto Rican!"). Sullivan himself once commented that it took him six years to "thaw out" in front of the camera. How in God's name did this man stay on the air for more than two decades? ✦ Simple: Where we now skip nervously through a bewildering agora of 500 specialty channels, *Ed Sullivan* packed it all into one hour on Sunday nights at eight. The very first broadcast of *Toast of the Town*, on June 20, 1948 (the name wasn't changed to *The Ed Sullivan Show* until 1955), set the standard for the host's weirdly polyglot mix of talent: the hot young comedy duo of Dean Martin and Jerry Lewis, concert pianist Eugene List, Broadway songwriters Richard Rodgers and Oscar Hammerstein II, boxing referee Ruby Goldstein, singing fireman John Kokoman, and the Toastette dancers. ✦ And it only got stranger and more marvelous as the years rolled on. Tune into CBS on a Sunday night and you might find the Bolshoi Ballet, or 17-year-old Liza Minnelli, or Albert Schweitzer playing an organ solo from his African mission, or scenes from the latest Broadway smash, or a demented Italian mouse-puppet called Topo Gigio (who appeared over 50 times, more than any other act). ✦ And of course, in two freeze-frame moments of pop-culture glory, Elvis Presley and the Beatles. It's worth noting that Sullivan passed on Elvis at first and paid dearly for it, coughing up $50,000 in 1956 for Presley's three appearances (two in '56, one in '57) after the singer had wowed the nation on Steve Allen's show (Col. Parker had originally asked for $5,000). Was it worth the money? With 60 million viewers—83 percent of everyone watching TV—what do you think? Over the course of 1,087 "rilly big shews" from 1948 to 1971, Sullivan both tailored the variety format to a new medium and saw its demise. The former New York sportswriter and gossip columnist knew that ultimate power was in the hands of the viewer ("This isn't vaudeville," he said. "People flip that knob") and consequently front-loaded his big acts into the opening minutes of the show, promising audiences they'd return later. But as the '60s rolled into the '70s, younger viewers kept right on flipping. "I was on the ground floor of radio and dropped out of it like a dope," Sullivan had once presciently commented. "Now I'm on the ground floor of TV, and I'm not giving up my lease until the landlord evicts me." On June 8, 1971, CBS canceled that lease. Three years later, Mr. Sunday Night was dead. —TY BURR/PHOTOGRAPHY BY ALLAN GRANT

THE TWILIGHT ZONE

SUBMITTED FOR YOUR APPROVAL: ROD SERLING'S SURREAL WORLD (WHERE NOTHING IS AS IT SEEMS)

*

THE TELEVISION INDUSTRY wasn't quite sure what Rod Serling was up to with his new show. Having won Emmys for writing serious teleplays like 1955's "Patterns" and 1956's "Requiem for a Heavyweight"—the latter considered by many to be the single finest drama of TV's Golden Age—Serling was now turning his energies to producing and writing...a sci-fi series. Comic-book stuff, figured the pundits. "You've given up writing anything important for television, right?" Mike Wallace asked Serling in an interview shortly before *The Twilight Zone* premiere. ✦ On the contrary. The original *Twilight Zone*, which ran on CBS from 1959 to 1964, lodged so deeply in the craniums of the baby-boom generation that you can still get a nervous laugh out of anyone just by imitating

its pinprick theme music. Each episode was a tautly written morality play in which supernatural and sci-fi elements tease out the characters' good or evil. A man who despises machines is attacked by his home appliances. An antisocial bookworm survives a nuclear holocaust and has all the time he needs to read—until his glasses break. A weary commuter steps off a train into what seems a picture-perfect town; in reality, he's jumping to his death. ✦ Perhaps the signal episode of *Twilight Zone* is "The Eye of the Beholder." It's the one about the distraught, supposedly deformed woman whose plastic surgery doesn't take; when we finally see her face, she's beautiful—it's the doctors and everyone else who are mutants. Throughout the series, Serling played to the rising counterculture by hinting that, behind its mask, our smug normality wasn't all that normal. ✦ In truth, Serling chose the sci-fi genre because it was the only place he could be subversive without scaring off sponsors. He had long strained against the straitjacket of TV's blandness: After a *Studio One* drama about the Senate had been watered down, he groused, "I probably would have had a much more adult play had I...put it in the year 2057 and peopled the Senate with robots." ✦ That's why *The Twilight Zone* remains one of TV's classics: Even if Serling hadn't hosted it, his terse urgency would still have shone through every script (he wrote more than half). Though he died at age 50 in 1975 from complications following open-heart surgery, Serling's influence is pervasive in the New Paranoia of the late '90s. Decades before *The X-Files*, Rod Serling knew you had to go out there to find the truth. —TB

JUST THE FACTS

THE TWILIGHT ZONE

YEARS ON AIR 1959–64

TOP NIELSEN CHARTING Never cracked the top 35

EMMYS WON 4

ORIGINAL CASTING Orson Welles was the preferred choice for host.

GROUNDBREAKING MOMENT One of the first network shows to say something critical about the U.S. involvement in Vietnam (in 1963!).

AUTHOR, AUTHOR Rod Serling was reputed to write TV scripts in as little as four hours and eventually completed more than 200, including 92 of the 156 *Twilight Zone* episodes. He also wrote the adapted screenplays for *The Planet of the Apes* and *Seven Days in May*.

THE TWILIGHT OF HIS LIFE In the years after *Zone* was canceled, Serling was haunted by the idea that he was a has-been. He accepted almost any offer, from game shows to commercials for Crest and Echo floor wax.

JUST THE FACTS

GUNSMOKE

YEARS ON AIR 1955–75

TOP NIELSEN CHARTING 1st (1957–61); in the top 20 for 15 years (1956–64, 1967–74)

EMMYS WON 5

HOW IT ALL BEGAN William Conrad (who would later narrate *The Fugitive* and star in *Cannon* and *Jake and the Fatman*) voiced the role of lawman Dillon in the original radio series.

HOW THE ROLE WAS WON John Wayne, who suggested Arness for the part of Matt Dillon, also introduced the premier episode.

SMALL WORLD Arness is the brother of *Mission: Impossible* star Peter Graves.

WESTWARD HO In the radio version of *Gunsmoke*, it was implied that Miss Kitty was a prostitute, but on TV, her virtue was restored. Actress Blake almost lost her job once for referring to her character as a "tramp."

SLIGHTLY EMBARRASSING PREVIOUS CAREER HIGHLIGHTS Before *Gunsmoke*, Arness' biggest roles had been as an arctic ice monster in *The Thing* (1951) and as a giant carrot in *Them!* (1954).

KEEPING THE STAR HAPPY As Arness gained more control over the show, he arranged the shooting schedule so he didn't have to work more than three days a week.

KEEPING THE STAR IN THE PICTURE Directors sometimes had to stand the 6-foot-7-inch Arness in a hole to keep his face in the same frame as the other actors.

THAT WAS A CLOSE ONE *Gunsmoke* was canceled in 1967 after years of slipping ratings. But after a huge public outcry, CBS honcho William Paley intervened, ordering programmers to reinstate the show in a new time slot. It quickly returned to the top 10 and ran for eight more years.

GUNSMOKE

FOR 20 YEARS, MARSHAL MATT DILLON AND MISS KITTY MADE DODGE CITY—AND THIS OLD WEST MORALITY PLAY—THE PLACE TO BE

16

TALK ABOUT BIG GUNS. For 20 years (1955-75), *Gunsmoke* towered above other TV Westerns in much the same way that its star, the 6-foot-7-inch James Arness, dwarfed everyone around him. And *Gunsmoke*'s legend still stands tall. The show, which had begun as a radio program, holds the distinction of being the longest-running prime-time television series of all time. ✦ Much of the appeal of *Gunsmoke*, which was set in the rough-and-tumble frontier town of Dodge City, Kan., circa 1873, was due to the marvelous chemistry that existed among the cast members. Arness' Marshal Matt Dillon was a man's man to rival John Wayne (who, in fact, had originally been offered—and turned down—the role of Dillon) and was the glue that held Dodge together. After him came the venerable, irascible physician Doc Adams (Milburn Stone); bighearted, limp-along deputy Chester Goode (Dennis Weaver); and, following Weaver's departure in 1964, his perpetually unshaven replacement, Festus Haggen (Ken Curtis), a backward, lovable mountain man. A young Burt Reynolds was also around for three seasons (1962-65), portraying the half-Indian blacksmith Quint Asper. ✦ To offset all that testosterone there was the lovely Kitty Russell (*Miss* Kitty to you, pardner). Played by Amanda Blake, Kitty owned Dodge City's favorite watering hole, the Long Branch Saloon, and was perhaps the show's most intriguing character. Not quite Dillon's girlfriend—the pair danced around each other in a coy, platonic two-step for the length of the show's run—Kitty was a strong, capable businesswoman, a pre-feminist role model who seemed to have more common sense than most of the men around her. She also carried a whiff of sin; although her on-screen behavior was almost always as proper as a schoolmarm's, many viewers suspected that this tough redhead, who resembled nothing so much as a well-heeled madam, knew a thing or two about the world's oldest profession. (Just what do you think was going on behind those closed upstairs doors at the Long Branch, anyway?) ✦ And yet, *Gunsmoke* was, above all, a highly moral show, one that dealt with timeless issues—love, greed, violence, power, inequity—in a primitive, Old West setting. Each week there was a showdown between good and evil (sometimes fought with guns, sometimes not), pitting Dillon or some other Dodge City resident against criminals, scoundrels, or low-life connivers. But the cowboy archetypes the show depicted somehow transcended cliché, becoming mythic forces unto themselves. More than two decades after its demise, the legacy of what was perhaps the quintessential TV Western still resonates like the echo of a pistol shot on a quiet, dusty street. —TOM SINCLAIR

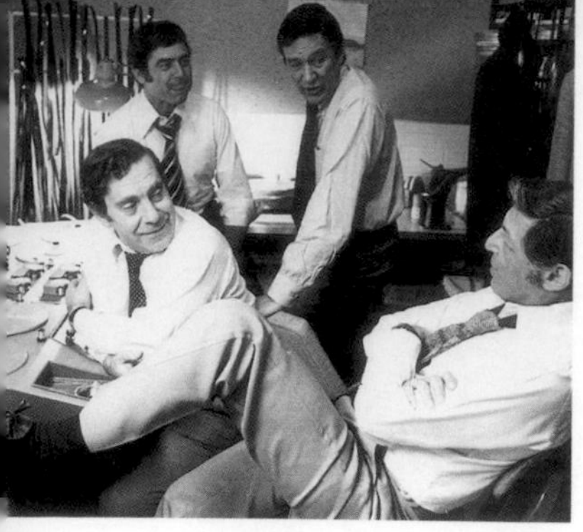

TICK-TICK-TICK. That sound has set countless scam artists and sleazy defense lawyers to trembling. For the rest of us, though, the famous stopwatch signals that we're in for an hour (or at least 52 minutes) of the hardest-hitting, smartest newsmagazine around. They did it first, and they do it the best. ✦ The brainchild of abrasive but astute producer Don Hewitt, *60 Minutes* arrived on air in 1968. "This is *60 Minutes*," intoned cohost Harry Reasoner. "It's kind of a magazine for television." That episode—featuring a report on the Nixon campaign and a story on tensions with big-city cops—tanked in the ratings. But in less than a decade, the show became a Sunday institution to rival football and church: It has stayed in the top 10 for more than 20 years. Spawned a vanload of imitators, from *Dateline* to *20/20*. Been lampooned by *Saturday Night Live*. Aired over 2,800 stories and made CBS more than a billion bucks. ✦ The secret? "Tell me a story" is Hewitt's mantra. Or, as he once said, the ratings could double "if we package reality as well as Hollywood packages fiction." ✦ Like a good movie, the show has clear-cut stars and the pace zips along. But most important, *60 Minutes* brims with conflict. Even after all these years, the aging journalists remain bulldog inquisitors, detectives, and ambush artists. Mike Wallace has exposed dozens of frauds, from a crooked cancer clinic to a jailhouse credit-card sham. A black-wigged Lesley Stahl nailed a story on Romanian babies for sale. Steve Kroft asked the hard questions of accused adulterer Bill Clinton in 1992. Sometimes, the conflicts have been *too* dicey, like Wallace's infamously censored 1995 interview with tobacco whistle-blower Jeffrey Wigand. ✦ Still, there's no question *60 Minutes* is best when it sticks to tough pieces. When it ventures into celeb profiles (everyone from Oprah Winfrey to Itzhak Perlman) or when Andy Rooney offers his rambling ruminations on waiters and safety tops, the results can be strangely unsatisfactory. But we forgive them these minor flaws. As *Seinfeld*'s Elaine said of the show: It's our Sunday ritual. We need it to unwind. —AJJ

17

60 MINUTES

AFTER 30 YEARS, THE GRANDDADDY OF NEWSMAGS IS STILL ALIVE AND TICKING

18

THE THORNY STAND-UP BLOSSOMED INTO A BLUE-COLLAR STANDOUT

ROSEANN

COMMENCING HER CAREER as Roseanne Barr, a stand-up comic with a sardonic attitude and a mocking reference to her true-life housewifely self as a "domestic goddess," the nightclub performer went the way of many comedians and was offered her own show. Pretty quickly, however, it became clear that this Roseanne wasn't going to be shaped and molded by network suits and veteran comedy writers. She turned *Roseanne* into a kitchen-sink sitcom whose grunginess hadn't been seen on television since *The Honeymooners*, and imbued it with a nascent feminism that grew stronger with each season. ✦ Surrounding herself with a strong, supple cast that included John Goodman as her long-suffering, job-hopping husband, Laurie Metcalf as her mooncalf sister, and Sara Gilbert as the era's most finely etched miserable teen, Roseanne scored a hit from the git-go. Viewers responded to her lower-middle-class manifestos of pride because they were enlivened by a tough, blunt humor. Since the star ran through writers and producers the way Cher does wigs, she must ultimately be given the credit for the series' unique combination of realism and idealism. ✦ And she must therefore also shoulder the blame for the dispirited mess *Roseanne* became in its last two seasons on ABC. When the Conner family won the lottery and became nouveau riche, reality went out the window, and the show degenerated into self-indulgent foolishness. Forget *Roseanne*'s final days and remember, in syndication, its early, earthy triumph. —KT

JUST THE FACTS

60 MINUTES

YEARS ON AIR 1968–present

TOP NIELSEN CHARTING 1st (It is the only program to be 1st in three different decades: the '70s, '80s, and '90s.)

EMMYS WON 63

SHOW THEM THE MONEY The most lucrative program in TV history, *60 Minutes* has made well over $1 billion for CBS and during some years has pulled in as much as 50 percent of its broadcast revenue.

TEMPUS FUGIT Three kinds of stopwatches have been used over the years on *60 Minutes*. The first one was gold and appeared only on the closing credits.

HUMBLE BEGINNINGS *60 Minutes* debuted opposite powerhouse *Marcus Welby, M.D.*, and finished its first season dead last in the ratings.

WHAT DID THEY KNOW? In an early review, *Variety* wrote: "If it had been a newspaper, it would not have sold many copies. The stories were dated and the magazine format, lifted from print, pretentious."

ROSEANNE

YEARS ON AIR 1988–97

TOP NIELSEN CHARTING 1st (1988–89, 1989–90); in top 10 for six seasons

EMMYS WON 4

PRESCIENT CASTING George Clooney as Booker Brooks, Roseanne's randy foreman at Wellman Plastics

WHAT DID THEY KNOW? "That a badly written series jammed with post-feminist pop-over clichés featuring a star who possesses the minimal requirements of acting should meet with such swift public approval suggests something about our present state of TV comedy that borders the runic." –*Los Angeles Times*, Dec. 11, 1988

UN-FUNNY BUSINESS After one turbulent year, exec producer Jeff Harris announced his resignation with an ad in *Daily Variety* that read in part: "My wife and I have decided to share a vacation in the relative peace and quiet of Beirut." Roseanne's reply: "Yeah, they're not gonna think you're very funny in Beirut either."

DALLAS

MEAN AS A TEXAS TWISTER, J.R. SOAPED UP PRIME TIME

IN THE SUMMER OF 1980, with Jimmy Carter running for reelection against an affable former actor named Ronald Reagan, a novelty campaign button began appearing: "J.R. for president," it said over the devilishly grinning, cowboy-hatted face of Larry Hagman. ✦ No question about it—all of America had J.R. on the brain. A month or so earlier, millions had been plunged into one of the greatest national guessing games of all time by a cliff-hanger season ender to the addictively popular prime-time soap opera *Dallas*. The last thing viewers saw was a freeze-frame of the gleefully amoral Texas tycoon J.R. Ewing (Hagman) lying unconscious in his Ewing Oil corporate office, shot by...well, who knew? ✦ It wasn't until Nov. 21, five episodes into the new season (and nearly three weeks after Reagan's landslide victory), that the delicious torment of "Who shot J.R.?" finally ended. The shooter's identity: J.R.'s sister-in-law, Kristin Shepard (Mary Crosby), with whom he had had a nasty little affair (weren't they all?). The episode naming Bing Crosby's angel-faced daughter as the would-be killer raked in Texas-size ratings (in fact, the highest in TV history, until *M*A*S*H*'s finale in 1983). ✦ It was the crowning glory for a drama that had America glued to its feverish mix of boardroom—and bedroom—shenanigans. Soon after the series debuted in 1978, it became clear that J.R. (aptly described by TIME magazine as "that human oil slick") was one of the most deliciously wicked villains in TV history. He was, in fact, an ideal cultural touchstone for that era: rich as Croesus, impervious to any kind of "national malaise," he tirelessly lied, schemed, and philandered. "Once you give up integrity, the rest is a piece of cake," J.R. said. It was the joy he took in his own villainy, as much as his naked lust for money and power, that viewers thrilled to. As the Reagan era took off, setting the stage for the Michael Milkens and Ivan Boeskys, it was almost like J.R. was leading the way. —NB/PHOTOGRAPH BY BARRY STAVER

19

SESAME STREET

WITH THIS RIP-ROARING KID-FEST, LEARNING WAS AS FUN AND EASY AS 1-2-3

20

HOW DO YOU GET A KID to swallow something icky? You put it on a brightly colored spoon and fly it around the room like an airplane while making keen barnstorming noises. In other words, you make a game out of it. And that's exactly what *Sesame Street* did with education: It dolled up learning and made it fun. ✦ This richly imaginative series, arguably the most ambitious educational experiment ever mounted on TV, is so engrained in the global culture (forget pop culture, this is *way* bigger than that) that to imagine a world without Kermit the Frog is...well, inhuman. ✦ Conceived by then-public TV producer Joan Ganz Cooney in 1968, *Sesame Street* was a radical departure from the lazy, hazy ways of *Mister Rogers' Neighborhood.* Combining the frenzied appeal of *Rowan and Martin's Laugh-In* with the repetitive lure of TV commercials, *Street* boasted a snappy style and catchy tunes—but what really made the show fly into the hearts of children in 120 countries was Jim Henson's Muppets. When the Muppet maestro decided to take up residence in the brownstone at 123 Sesame St., Kermit, Big Bird, Oscar the Grouch, Ernie, Bert, Cookie Monster, and countless others became neighbors to the kids of the world. ✦ While the Muppets indulged young viewers' flights of fancy—teaching them the length of an earthworm, say, or the strength of Cookie Monster's appetite—the multiethnic human cast reflected the varied hues of *Sesame Street*'s target viewers: urban youth. "The audience we wanted to reach was often trapped in an apartment and the action was out on the street," says Jon Stone, the show's first head writer. And reach them they did. According to one survey, *Sesame Street* plays to 92 percent of children in low-income households. ✦ In the years since *Sesame Street* premiered, tons of accolades have been heaped upon it, and scores of celebs (including Glenn Close, Whoopi Goldberg, Ray Charles, and Danny DeVito) have visited the playful patch of pavement. But the true measure of its success can be found in the hearts and minds of the kids who have grown up and taken their place in a society formed, in part, through the eternal lessons taught on *Sesame Street.* It's not easy being evergreen, but it's worth it. —MARC BERNARDIN

JUST THE FACTS

DALLAS

YEARS ON AIR
1978–91

TOP NIELSEN CHARTING
1st (1980–81, 1981–82, 1983–84); "Who Shot J.R.?" had then-largest TV audience in history; nearly 76 percent of all viewers tuned in.

EMMYS WON 3

THE ROAD NOT TAKEN
At the time he was offered the role of J.R., Hagman was also asked to star opposite Joe Namath in *The Waverly Wonders*, which lasted only one month. He was leaning toward the latter when his wife talked him into *Dallas*.

HOT SPOT In the 1980s, Southfork became the No. 1 tourist attraction in Dallas, displacing the Texas Schoolbook Depository.

LOST IN TRANSLATION
Dallas was a hit in 90 of the 91 countries in which it was syndicated. The holdout? Japan.

SPIN-OFFS *Knots Landing* and a 1986 TV movie, *Dallas: The Early Years*

SESAME STREET

YEARS ON AIR
1969–present

TOP NIELSEN CHARTING Not available

EMMYS WON 77

ORIGINAL TITLE
The Preschool Educational Television Show

BUM RAP Early critics said *Sesame Street* would stunt children's attention spans.

PRODUCTION NOTES
Show stays fresh by recycling programming ideas every three years, by which time a new group of kids is watching.

THE EXTENT OF ITS SUCCESS American teachers now expect children to arrive on the first day of school knowing the basics about letters, numbers, and language. "Kindergarten now does what first grade used to do," Cooney has said, "and I think that's directly due to *Sesame Street*."

WHAT DO WE ASK OF A BOX THAT SITS IN OUR LIVING ROOMS and greets us as we come home from wrestling with the outside world? Mostly, we ask to be soothed and diverted and surprised. Since these are all things at which comedy excels, it's hardly coincidental that the sitcom has become the medium's signal genre, to the point where laugh tracks sometimes seem to hover over our daily conversations. But if almost all television comedy serves the same rock-bottom purpose—to explain and ease social friction by playing various types against each other (okay, okay, and to make us laugh)—the three primary schools of sitcoms go about it differently. In short: Family comedies soothe, ensemble comedies divert, and those rare shows that are the product of a unique comic sensibility surprise and delight us. ✦ It's the family comedies that may tell us the most about ourselves—or about how we want to see ourselves. That's a big difference, as the charming, unreal banalities of '50s classics like *The Adventures of Ozzie* and *Harriet* and *Leave It to Beaver* prove. "We always laughed at what Ward was supposed to do for a living," *Beaver* costar Barbara Billingsley recalled in later years. "We never knew." As the '60s kicked in, you could feel the seams stretching in shows like *Bewitched*, where Mom was a witch and God forbid the neighbors should find out. With the '70s and *All in the Family* (see the Top 20 chapter on page 6), sitcom families were finally allowed to argue, and by the '80s, everything was topsy-turvy: On *Family Ties*, it was the *kids* who were the straight-arrows. It was only with *The Cosby Show* that the sitcom family reclaimed the center. ✦ Ensemble comedies have tended to focus on the workplace and are thus comparatively mature. *The Dick Van Dyke Show*'s the pioneer here; creator Carl Reiner purposely set out to write a show where "you saw where the man worked before he walked in and said, 'Hi, honey, I'm home!' " But it was *The Mary Tyler Moore Show* (see the Top 20) that carved the rules to which ensemble comedies still hew. The variations are infinite: *Barney Miller* is set in a precinct house, *Taxi* among cabbies, *Friends* amongst friends. The current best of breed is *Frasier*, which manages to fuse the family sitcom and workplace farce in ways that satisfyingly deepen both. ✦ We reserve our awe, however, for those shows that bottle singular genius. To watch *The Jack Benny Show* is to luxuriate in one man's Olympian gift for comic timing. To laugh at Bullwinkle the moose in *Rocky and His Friends* is to appreciate Jay Ward's goofy, eccentric savvy. If not for *Sanford and Son*, we'd know Redd Foxx only through out-of-print, under-the-counter comedy albums. As for *Bob Newhart*—well, his precisely calibrated, expertly judged reactions to the world's absurdities could flower only on TV. ✦ There are a few anomalies included in this chapter—ruptures that injected the entropic sitcom universe with new and needed energy. If England's *Monty Python's Flying Circus* still looks more anarchic than anything that has ever originated here, the parodic *Mary Hartman, Mary Hartman* came awfully close. And at the end we've tossed in a section on the best game shows because, in a weird way, they capture the human comedy—the greed, the ambition, the frenzied grab for the buzzer—better than any sitcom. Here, at last, is a format to soothe, divert, and surprise—and hand out lovely Cracker Jack prizes in the bargain. —TY BURR

PHOTOGRAPH BY NOLA LÓPEZ

COMEDIES

TV'S SMARTEST SITCOM BROUGHT HIGHBROW HUMOR INTO THE MEDIUM, RAISED PUT-DOWNS TO AN ART...AND SOMETIMES GAVE A SCRUFFY TERRIER THE LAST WORD

FRASIER

NO MATTER THAT *The George Wendt Show, The Tortellis*, and *Ink* all tanked. Never mind that psychiatrist Frasier Crane had told his beloved *Cheers* chums that his parents were both research scientists, were both dead, and that he was an only child. When *Frasier* debuted on NBC in 1993, all was forgiven: Reviewers and viewers alike immediately accepted the show's premise and characters as if they were new old friends. ✦ In a sense, they were. One of *Frasier*'s canniest tricks was to give its prissy hero an even prissier foil in the person of younger brother (and Jungian to Frasier's Freudian) Niles Crane. It's no coincidence that their fraternal rivalry echoes the interplay between Frasier and his two main loves, Diane and Lilith, on *Cheers*: In all three cases, an overeducated, pompous bore is made startlingly human by comparison. ✦ That said, actors Kelsey Grammer and David Hyde Pierce have taken brotherly love to heights never seen before in sitcom land: With every muttered bon mot and withering glare, you can see these guys as adolescents, trying to top each other at the science fair. *Frasier*'s scripts are among the medium's most literate, and the ensemble cast is a glory, what with John Mahoney's gruff dad, Peri Gilpin's seen-it-all Roz, and Jane Leeves' properly sultry Daphne (of whom Niles once moaned, "Oh, why couldn't you have just hired some beefy, Eastern European scrubwoman who reeked of ammonia instead of Venus herself?"). Hell, even the dog's a natural. But, in the end, it's Grammer and Pierce who make *Frasier* one for the ages, reminding us that elitism has its roots in insecurity and that wine lists are useless unless you can browbeat somebody—preferably family—with them. —TY BURR

JUST THE FACTS

FRASIER

YEARS ON AIR
1993–present

TOP NIELSEN CHARTING
7th (its first season)

EMMYS WON
16, including Outstanding Comedy four years in a row

ORIGINS
Successful spin-off of *Cheers'* Frasier Crane character

NON-PRESCIENT CASTING
Lisa Kudrow, cast to play sassy radio producer Roz, was replaced by Peri Gilpin when she and Grammer failed to catch fire together. (Kudrow snared her *Friends* role two years later.)

MADNESS IN THE METHOD
Grammer tries to keep his performances fresh by waiting until a few minutes before he shoots a scene to learn his lines.

BIRTHRIGHTS
Jane Leeves (who plays Manchester-born Daphne Moon) isn't actually from Manchester; she's from the London suburb of East Grinstead. John Mahoney (who plays the Seattle-born Martin Crane) isn't actually from Seattle; he's from Manchester, England (he emigrated to the U.S. as a teen).

OTHER VOICES, OTHER ROOMS
On *Frasier*, major stars (Jodie Foster, Carrie Fisher, Kevin Bacon, Lily Tomlin, Mel Brooks, Sandra Dee, Patty Hearst, Jay Leno) often do cameos in which their voices are heard, but they're never seen.

JUSTTHEFACTS

THE WONDER YEARS

YEARS ON AIR 1988–93

TOP NIELSEN CHARTING 8th (1989–90)

EMMYS WON 5; Savage, 12, was youngest best actor nominee ever.

MILK MONEY One reason the producers ended the show was that as Kevin entered his teens (and got a driver's license) they had to shoot more on location, bringing the per-episode cost to a hefty $1.2 million.

NOT-SO-HEAVY PETTING When the producers had Kevin touch a girl's breast in the fourth season, censors made them cut 1.5 seconds of footage. Exec producer Michael Dinner recalled being told: "No one in the history of television at 8 p.m. has ever touched a breast."

PRESCIENT CASTING Alicia Silverstone was Kevin's "dream date" in a 1992 episode; David Schwimmer played sister Karen's boyfriend, Michael.

LEAVE IT TO BEAVER

YEARS ON AIR 1957–63

TOP NIELSEN CHARTING Never cracked top 35.

EMMYS WON 0

ORIGINAL TITLE The CBS pilot was first called *Wally and Beaver*, but to sponsor Remington Rand, that sounded like a nature show, so it was rechristened *It's a Small World* before the final title.

WHY THE NICKNAME? Writers Joe Connelly and Bob Mosher thought *Beaver* connot character who was "all

CAST NOTES Beaumon Methodist preacher who ous acting experience mostly in religious films retired to Minnesota to Christmas trees.

KEEPING THE SUBURB Osmond grew up to be

PRESCIENT CASTING In 1957 pilot, Frankie (who later morph into Eddie was played by Harry Sh

THE WONDER YEARS

BOY'S LIFE: FOR A KID NAMED KEVIN, IT WASN'T ALL FUN AND GAMES

HERE WAS THE FIRST SERIES about kids done by people who actually had *been* kids—or so it seemed, such was the power of its humor and insight. Charting the life of a middle American boy named Kevin in the late '60s and early '70s, the ABC series adroitly captured the contradictory rush of emotions—sometimes ecstatic, sometimes wrenching—that course through a real 12-year-old's mind as he faces the world. ✦ The scenes are vintage small-town boy: When Kevin (played with unusual deftness by Fred Savage) visits the factory where his father is a manager, he swells with pride as Dad chews out subordinates for slacking off—but later is crushed to hear his dad get a similar tongue-lashing from his boss. When Kevin is paired with the dowdiest girl at a school dance, he finds he actually likes her—but when his friends later poke fun at her, he remains silent. "In seventh grade, who you are is what other seventh-graders say you are," explains the grown-up Kevin (narrator Daniel Stern, who, though never seen, acted as a poignant pundit, bringing viewers inside the main character's mind as no show had before). ✦ Unfortunately, though, the show had a built-in biological clock: How wondrous would the adolescent years be when Kevin had to cope with issues like drugs and sex? The producers had always joked that they would end the show when the period music became disco, but it actually didn't last *that* long. In 1993 (1973 in the show's time), *The Wonder Years* aired its last episode. Kevin, now 17, grew disgusted with a job at his dad's factory and walked out—into the arms of his girlfriend Winnie. But for five years, his wonders—and ours—had never ceased.

—MATTHEW McCANN FENTON / PHOTOGRAPH BY BOB D'AMICO

WHEN BABY BOOMERS recall their childhood, they should consider carefully. It may not be their own suburban upbringing they're dreaming of, but the one they shared with a scrappy Everykid named Beaver. ✦ If only families had been as idyllic as *Leave It to Beaver*'s Cleaver clan—but no dad was ever as levelheaded as Ward (Hugh Beaumont), moms didn't vacuum in pearls and shirtwaist dresses like June (Barbara Billingsley), and older brothers weren't as dopily protective as Wally (Tony Dow). ✦ And then, of course, there was the always-lovable Beav himself. With his puckish, round face, Jerry Mathers was like a cartoon Disney animal come to life. And no matter what his high jinks—being trapped in a giant billboard coffee cup, giving himself a wretched haircut—it was guaranteed that Ward and June would calmly instill a lesson in his noggin. Sound too saccharine? Rest assured there were a few flies in the ointment, like Wally's two best friends, the aptly named Lumpy Rutherford (Frank Bank) and the two-faced Eddie Haskell (Ken Osmond), who fooled no one with his unctuous compliments ("You look *particularly* lovely today, Mrs. Cleaver"). ✦ Inevitably, Mathers grew from adorable 9-year-old to gangly, croaky-voiced pubescent and the show lost its childish appeal. But the Beav—like Mickey Rooney's Andy Hardy before him and *The Wonder Years'* Fred Savage 30 years later—put a face on American childhood that endures to this day.

—JOE NEUMAIER / PHOTOGRAPH BY BOB WILLOUGHBY

LEAVE IT TO BEAVER

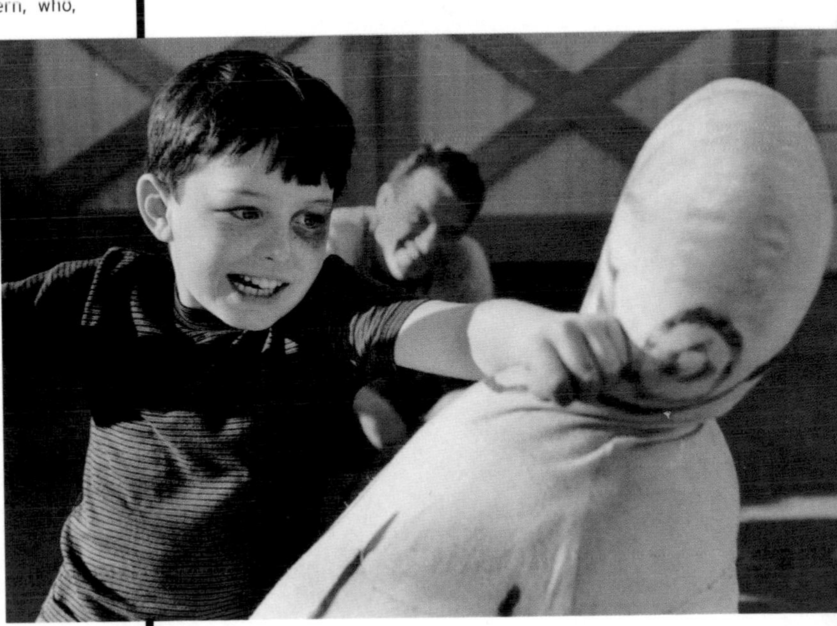

WE STILL LIKE THIS IKE-ERA MUNCHKIN

THE ODD COUPLE

HOW DO TWO OPPOSITES ATTRACT LEGIONS OF FANS? IT'S SIMPLE, SIMON.

LONG BEFORE JERRY SEINFELD and George Costanza sat around a New York City apartment bantering about Nothing, Tony Randall's single-thin-and-neat Felix Unger and Jack Klugman's raging-id Oscar Madison patented the act. Okay, so Jack Lemmon and Walter Matthau played the roles first in the 1968 film, but it's a testament to Randall and Klugman's prodigious talents that we instantly picture their faces whenever we hear the words *The Odd Couple*. ✦ Fastidious photographer Felix and slobby sportswriter Oscar were divorced men sharing a bachelor pad out of sheer necessity. Sure, they drove each other crazy, but they couldn't live without each other. In the pre-feminist culture in which these guys were raised, Felix fulfilled the traditional role of the wife, cooking and cleaning, while Oscar was the aggressive, socially graceless husband (how different this sitcom might have been in the age of *Ellen*). ✦ In some ways a snapshot of the early '70s—with guest stars like loudmouthed sportscaster Howard Cosell and male-chauvinist tennis bum Bobby Riggs—*The Odd Couple* still maintained a timeless quality in its scripts (some penned by executive producer Garry Marshall, whose sister, Penny, played Oscar's secretary, Myrna). Perhaps that's why its humor has held up so well over the years; the series proved more popular in syndication than it ever was during its original ABC run. Viewed today, the show seems fresher and funnier than ever. After nearly 30 years, we're still awed by this couple. —BF

THE ABBOTT AND COSTELLO SHOW

SURE, SEINFELD'S GREAT—BUT WHO WAS ON FIRST?

MOST OF THE WORLD KNOWS the legendary comedy duo primarily from their movie work—Bud Abbott and Lou Costello, after all, made 38 films together and were once Hollywood's premier marquee draw. But, aesthetically at least, it was in their syndicated sitcom (one of TV's very *first*, by the way) that Bud and Lou forged their resonant us-against-the-world trademark style. ✦ Talk about "no hugging, no learning": This is where the jaundiced *Seinfeld*ian ethos truly originated. Sure, there was no shortage of pratfalls and pie-faces in the repertoire of 52 half-hour shorts that made up Bud and Lou's series—but there was also something much more audacious and dark going on. *The Abbott and Costello Show*'s slapstick was underlined by a certain sardonicism, as Bud and Lou faced a world (well, a city, anyway) full of people gleefully making life difficult for them, whether it was dim-witted buttinsky Mike the Cop, neighborhood vendor Bacciagalupe, evil man-child Stinky (played to acid, foppic perfection by Stooge-to-be Joe Besser), or vindictive landlord Sid Fields. In fact, with the exception of their gal pal, Hillary Brooke, Bud and Lou seemed to bring out the sociopath in everyone, invariably ending up fleeced, debased, or brutalized. ✦ Dialogue came in punchy, rat-a-tat-tat exchanges, with insults and malapropisms ricocheting from character to character, as the visual (via some very crafty editing) raced to keep up with the aural. Witness the classic "He's positive!" scene, in which a routine reply to a judge whips an entire courtroom into a frenzy. And hey, in what other universe could you risk life and limb simply by uttering the words "Niagara Falls" to the wrong person? —MF

JUST THE FACTS

THE ODD COUPLE

YEARS ON AIR
1970–75

TOP NIELSEN CHARTING
36th (1972–73)

EMMYS WON 3

ORIGINAL CASTING
Producers wanted Art Carney and Martin Balsam. ABC wanted Randall and Mickey Rooney.

INSPIRATION
Neil Simon based his play on his Oscar-like brother, Danny.

ART KINDA IMITATES LIFE
Klugman's real-life wife, Brett Somers, played his ex-wife, Blanche.

NO KIDDING
In Simon's original play, both Oscar and Felix had children. But ABC nixed kids for the show, saying that according to their standards, divorced people didn't have children. Eventually, ABC let children be written into the script for Felix.

SPIN-OFFS
The New Odd Couple (a 1982–83 remake with black actors); *The Oddball Couple*, a 1975–77 animated series about a sloppy dog and tidy cat.

THE ABBOTT AND COSTELLO SHOW

YEARS ON AIR
1951–53

TOP NIELSEN CHARTING
Not available

BITING THE HAND THAT FEEDS YOU
Bingo the Chimp was fired in the second season for biting Lou.

NO FOOLISH CONSISTENCY HERE
Characters changed occupations almost weekly, as the needs of each episode demanded. For instance, Hillary, Lou's girlfriend from across the hall, was variously a nurse, a dental assistant, and a secretary.

SILENT PARTNER
It was common knowledge that the two weren't the best of friends off the set. Costello reportedly demanded–and got–60 percent of the pair's take.

SPIN-OFFS
An animated series, *The Abbott and Costello Show* (produced by Hanna-Barbera), was one of the first cartoons based on real people; it used Abbott's voice.

JUST THE FACTS

HOWDY DOODY

YEARS ON AIR
1947–60

TOP NIELSEN CHARTING
Never ranked in top 25

EMMYS WON 0

AS AMERICAN AS APPLE PIE The second Howdy Doody had 48 freckles, one for each state of the Union. (The first was replaced when the original puppeteer left after a merchandising dispute.)

HIDDEN MEANINGS The Chief Thunderthud character is supposed to be the leader of the fictive Ooragnak tribe of Indians. The name is *kangaroo* spelled backward.

PRESCIENT ARGOT The show introduced the word *kawabonga* as an exclamation of surprise or exasperation.

AFTER BIRTH Tickets to the show were so scarce that pregnant mothers would try to reserve in advance seats for their unborn children.

SUBSEQUENT CAREER HIGHLIGHTS More than a decade after the show left the air, Howdy made a cameo appearance (as himself) on *Happy Days*.

ROCKY AND HIS FRIENDS

YEARS ON AIR
1959–61

TOP NIELSEN CHARTING
Not available

EMMYS WON 0

WHERE THEY GOT THE NAME *Bullwinkle* comes from a Berkeley, Calif., car dealership near Ward's boyhood home.

OTHER CAREERS Ward graduated from Harvard Business School and returned to California to work in real estate.

SPIN-OFF Prime time's *The Bullwinkle Show*, which aired on NBC from 1961 to 1964, introduced such characters as Snidely Whiplash and Dudley Do-Right.

UNDER THE INFLUENCE In his thriller *Clear and Present Danger*, Tom Clancy made reference to a silent bomb—an explosive that could destroy entire communities without making a sound. He reportedly got the idea not from some highly placed government source but from a 1962 episode of *The Bullwinkle Show*. (On the show, the device was called "Hush-A-Boom.")

SO HE GAVE A WOODEN PERFORMANCE—THIS TV PIONEER STILL HAD YOUNG FANS ON A STRING

'HOWDY DOODY' WAS THE GREAT GRANDDADDY of kiddie shows. Adapted from a radio program called *Triple B Ranch*, the program, which debuted in 1947 under the name *Puppet Playhouse*, introduced an entire generation of young fans to the delights of the then-new medium of television. So popular was the show that at the height of its success, the singsong theme, "It's Howdy Doody Time," had a positively Pavlovian effect on anyone under age 10. ✦ *Howdy Doody* was the brainchild of Buffalo Bob Smith, who presided over the puppets and costumed humans of the scatologically named TV town of Doodyville, chief among them the wooden marionette of the show's title. Howdy was actually popular enough to be touted as a presidential candidate in 1948; after he threw his hat into the ring, 60,000 requests for "I'm for Howdy Doody" campaign buttons poured in—a figure that represented an estimated one third of all the TV sets in America at the time. ✦ Doodyville was populated by a diversity of characters, including Howdy's twin brother, Double Doody, and his sister, Heidi Doody, as well as human regulars like the mute clown, Clarabell (initially played by Bob Keeshan, who would later become Captain Kangaroo), and Princess Summerfall Winterspring, played by Judy Tyler. ✦ "The program is conducted at a noise level roughly five times that of [Milton] Berle," complained one critic in 1951, but kids reveled in all that cacophony. Sadly, the fun and games couldn't last forever. In 1956, after nearly a decade of running five times a week, *Howdy Doody* was consigned to a once-a-week Saturday-morning time slot. Though the show continued to be popular, the dynamic had changed, and with the original fan base grappling with adolescence, *Howdy Doody* time finally came to an end in September 1960. —TOM SINCLAIR

ROCKY AND HIS FRIENDS

A CARTOON SERIES THAT WAS MANY a baby boomer's introduction to satire and irony, this minimally animated show featured Rocket J. Squirrel (spunky, plucky, heroic) and Bullwinkle (dim-witted, clumsy, cowardly, but a poetry lover). The creation of writer-animator Jay Ward, ABC's *Rocky and His Friends* parodied old-fashioned movie serials that most of its audience probably didn't even remember existed. Heavy on puns and scrambled wordplay, the *Rocky* show pitted our heroes against runty spy Boris Badenov and his tall, slinky aide, Natasha, in Ward's ridiculing of Communist Cold War espionage. ✦ The half-hour show was also famous for its "Fractured Fairy Tales," often-witty turns on familiar stories narrated with plummy wryness by veteran character actor Edward Everett Horton, and the time-traveling sagas of Sherman (a not-too-bright little boy) and Mr. Peabody (a brilliant dog with horn-rim glasses). Mr. Peabody had a "Wayback Machine," a time-traveling device that permitted the duo to go back to various eras to generally muck things up and confuse major historical figures. In all this, Ward's achievement was to bring a wiseacre, *MAD*-magazine sensibility to cartoons—*Rocky* was the first animated series aimed at tickling grown-ups as much as the kiddies. —KT

KIDS (AND A FEW ADULTS) WENT NUTS FOR THE SQUIRREL-AND-MOOSE HEROES OF THIS COLD WAR CARTOON

THE JEFFERSONS

WITH GEORGE & CO., THE BUNKER MENTALITY WAS TURNED INSIDE OUT

PERHAPS THE BEST-KNOWN SPIN-OFF of *All in the Family* actually had a lot in common with that seminal series: Also produced by Norman Lear, CBS' *The Jeffersons* had a lead character, George Jefferson, who could match Archie Bunker insult for insult when it came to bigotry (George joked about playing "Pin the Tail on the Honky"). Like Edith Bunker, George's wife, Louise (a.k.a. Weezy), loved him despite all his bluster. And like Gloria Bunker Stivic, Lionel Jefferson pleaded with his father to be more open-minded. ✦ But this family wasn't just the Bunkers in blackface. After the Jeffersons moved on up to their "de-luxe apartment in the sky" on Manhattan's East Side, the sitcom broke new ground in its own right. As George (Sherman Hemsley) insulted the Willises—the first interracial married couple in sitcomland—we got a hint of something we hadn't seen on TV before: the anxieties of the black middle class. And, in George, we saw a positive role model—a successful black businessman who took no guff. ✦ The show spent three seasons in the top 10, but inevitably it grew softer, less relevant. George and Tom Willis bought a bar together; the smart-alecky maid, Florence, made it clear she liked George after all. By the end, *The Jeffersons* had been eclipsed by *Cosby*'s Huxtable clan, who seemed to live in a color-blind world. ✦ But thank goodness for *The Jeffersons*: Outrageous as it could be, its barbed humor made us think about the issues that arose when black Americans finally got a piece of the pie. —CAREN WEINER

THE NELSON RIDDLE: HOW DID A SEXY MOM AND SLACKER DAD SPAWN SUCH A BIG POP IDOL?

THE ADVENTURES OF OZZIE AND HARRIET

DECADES BEFORE 'THE TRUMAN SHOW' started everyone talking about the increasingly blurred lines between life and entertainment, ABC's *The Adventures of Ozzie and Harriet* invited viewers to tune in to the lives of a "real" American family each week. For 14 years, the country grew up and older watching Ozzie and Harriet Nelson and their two sons, David and Ricky, an unconditionally loving middle-class family living in idyllic comfort. For the Nelsons—on screen, at least—the good life was pain-free, and words like *abuse* and *dysfunctional* didn't exist. Still, an undercurrent of subtle subversion hummed beneath the program's placid surface. For starters, Ozzie seemed to be immune to regular work hours at his unidentified job, making him a ubiquitous father figure, albeit a bewildered one. And Harriet seemed just a tad too, well, sexy to be just a cooking-and-cleaning machine (in real life, she had been a singer in Ozzie's big band). Most crucially, though, there was the show's true star, Ricky, who evolved into a genuine proto-punk fronting his own rock & roll combo (which regularly played on the show). Though Ricky Nelson, Pop Star, has often been (unjustly) dismissed as a schlock teen idol in the Fabian mold, the truth is he played nearly as vital a role as Elvis in introducing mainstream America to the sound of amplified, beat-driven music. No less a rock & roll animal than Lou Reed has admitted being influenced by watching Ricky's band rockin' around the tube. The *Ozzie and Harriet*/Velvet Underground connection—hit your hipster friends with *that* one the next time they laugh at your love for the Nelsons. —TS

RSONS

AIR 1975–85

EN

6th (1981–82)

ON 3

CAREER HIGHLIGHTS
ame to acting late in
ints in the Air Force
ostal Service.

ES Florence wasn't
e a permanent char
audience's response
in the first show—"How come we overcame and nobody told me?"—was enough to make her a regular.

REPLACEMENT PARTS
Mike Evans had played Lionel on *All in the Family* and reprised the role during *The Jeffersons*' first season. But he was also a cocreator of *Good Times*, and the demands of both shows were too much. He was replaced as Lionel by actor Damon Evans (no relation), until 1979, when he returned to the role.

THE ADVENTURES OF OZZIE AND HARRIET

YEARS ON AIR 1952–66

TOP NIELSEN CHARTING 29th (1963–64)

EMMYS WON 0

CONTROL FREAKISHNESS
Nelson's unprecedented 10-year contract with ABC stated that he would write, direct, and produce most of the episodes.

SHOW THEM THE MONEY As boys, Ricky and David reportedly were each earning a higher salary than the U.S. President.

SYNCHRONICITY
The Nelsons' TV home was modeled on their actual house; after Ricky and David got married, both wives joined the cast.

KEEPING THE SPONSORS HAPPY
Many of the early scenes were filmed in the Nelson kitchen reportedly to show off the Hotpoint appliances.

SANFORD AND SON

PC? HARDLY. BUT THIS TRASH-TALKIN' JUNKYARD DOG KEPT US HOWLING.

TALK ABOUT QUESTIONABLE African-American role models: Fred Sanford (Redd Foxx), the main character in *Sanford and Son*, was a cantankerous, 65-year-old junk dealer given to lusting after women, insulting whites and non-black minorities, tippling "champipple" (champagne and Ripple), dreaming up scams, and generally making life miserable for his son, Lamont (Demond Wilson), a.k.a. "Dummy." Some critics carped that the show fostered the most noxious ethnic stereotypes since the heyday of *Amos 'n' Andy*—but for four of the five years it ran, this non-PC sitcom ranked among the top 10, scoring high marks with viewers of all colors. ✦ Originally touted as a sort of black *All in the Family* (both shows were produced by Norman Lear, who adapted the idea for *Sanford* from the British TV show *Steptoe and Son*), it featured a multiethnic cast that included, at various times, Lamont's Puerto Rican buddy Julio (Gregory Sierra) and the Asian handyman Ah Chew (Pat Morita). A variety of crotchety characters—such as Grady (Whitman Mayo), Bubba (Don Bexley), and the quick-tempered Aunt Esther ("Watch it, sucka!") Anderson (LaWanda Page)—floated in and out of the episodes, but it was the curiously affecting love-hate relationship between Foxx and Wilson that generated most of the laughs. (Who can forget Fred's recurring "heart attacks," usually triggered by Lamont's threats to leave home and accompanied by impassioned soliloquies to his dead wife—"I'm comin' to join you, Elizabeth. This is the big one!"?) ✦ While Foxx, a former X-rated stand-up comic, was clearly the show's linchpin, Wilson (who later retired from acting to become a minister) provided the perfect levelheaded foil for the old man's foolishness. Is it any wonder millions of fans gladly gave their hearts to these junk men each week? —TS

THE ANDY GRIFFITH SHOW

SOUTHERN COMFORT: IN MAYBERRY, FATHER REALLY DID KNOW BEST

THE GENTLEST, MOST KINDHEARTED sitcom ever, *The Andy Griffith Show* fashioned a kind of rural Eden out of the lives of the quiet, decent Mayberry, N.C., sheriff Andy Taylor (Griffith), his rambunctious little son, Opie (Ron Howard), plump Aunt Bee (Frances Bavier), and Andy's nervous, fumbling deputy, Barney Fife (Don Knotts). ✦ Griffith was doing a variation on the country-bumpkin persona he'd perfected in his comic routines and in *No Time for Sergeants* on Broadway, but as the series proceeded, the character deepened into a wise, humane fellow with a strong sense of justice and the equally strong feeling that the most important job in life is raising your child to be happy. Griffith became the straight man not only to the brilliantly dithery Knotts, but also to fumbling, fey Floyd the barber (Howard McNear), goofy gas attendant Gomer Pyle (Jim Nabors, who'd spin off to his own series), and Otis Campbell (Hal Smith), the town drunk—a stereotype who would never make it onto TV today, but who, in the world of Mayberry, was looked upon with tolerance and affection. ✦ Seen now, what's striking about *The Andy Griffith Show* is its soothing calmness (starting with that softly whistled theme song) and pervasive sense of decency. It holds up in reruns as a time capsule of a more innocent, trusting, and comforting time. —KT

ND SON

AIR 1972–77

N CHARTING
'3, 1974–75)

N 0

RABLE WHITENESS
The original pilot had
ghes as the father,
) as his son.

S FAMILIAR
ame is John Sanford.

A FOXX At various
ar refused to show
up for taping, citing ailments such as nervous exhaustion, hives, bone spurs, and torn cartilage. He later acknowledged fabricating the illnesses to wring concessions from the producers: a higher salary, a dressing room with a window, a golf cart to get him around NBC, and 25 percent of the show's net profits.

THIS IS THE BIG ONE Foxx, whose trademark shtick was a fake heart attack, collapsed with a fatal heart attack in 1991 on the set of *The Royal Family.*

THE ANDY GRIFFITH SHOW

YEARS ON AIR 1960–68

TOP NIELSEN CHARTING 1st (1967–68); never out of top 10

EMMYS WON 6, including 5 for Don Knotts

ONE FOR THE RECORD BOOKS One of only three series to go out on top of the Nielsens (the others: *I Love Lucy* and *Seinfeld*).

NO. 1 WITHOUT A BULLET Andy didn't wear a gun; Barney did—but carried only one bullet.

ORIGINS The CBS series began life as an episode of *The Danny Thomas Show*, in which Danny is arrested by Andy while driving through a small Southern town.

MEN OF FEW WORDS The scripts were substantially shorter than those of the average sitcom, to accommodate the characters' slow, drawling Southern accents.

SPIN-OFFS *Gomer Pyle, U.S.M.C.* (1964–70); *Mayberry R.F.D.* (1968–71)

JUSTTHEFACTS

THESE COPS WERE AS WACKY AS THEIR COLLARS—WHEN THEY GOT THEIR WOJO WORKING

BARNEY MILLER

AH, NEW YORK IN THE '70S. Graffiti-scarred subways, record crime, impending bankruptcy. At the movies, *Taxi Driver*'s Travis Bickle prophesies a "real rain" washing the scum off the streets, while *Kojak* portrays one detective's quest to cut a swath of righteousness through the harsh metropolis. Meanwhile, on *Barney Miller*, Jack Soo's Det. Nick Yemana mistakenly consumes some questionable brownies and goes off on a giddy, glazed-eyed reverie, pondering the "squish, squish" sound of his opening and closing eyelids. ✦ That priceless moment speaks volumes about this funky sitcom. Set in the detective squad room of the NYPD's 12th Precinct, a grungy, claustrophobic eyesore badly in need of a paint job (and, one sensed, a fumigation), *Barney Miller* managed to totally capture the eclectic, idiosyncratic sprawl of New York on its own little half-hour canvas. And it did it not only through the endless parade of pimps, perverts, thieves, and wackos who stewed in its holding cell but through the detectives themselves, a crew nearly as motley and off-kilter as their collars: They included Max Gail's neurotic, scatterbrained Wojohowicz; Steve Landesberg's acerbic Dietrich; Abe Vigoda's muttering, morose Fish; Ron Glass' suave, cocksure Harris; and James Gregory's loose-cannon Inspector Luger. And the calm center of all this craziness was squad captain Barney, played by straight man nonpareil Hal Linden. ✦ But ultimately, the most important character of all may have been the Big Apple itself, as evidenced by the lunatic interface between the good guys and the bad guys. What could have been mistaken for world-weary nonchalance on the part of the detectives was really an unspoken understanding of the criminals they dealt with, a knowing, we're-all-in-this-together vibe. And so we were, camped around the TV watching "Fun City" live up to its name. —MF

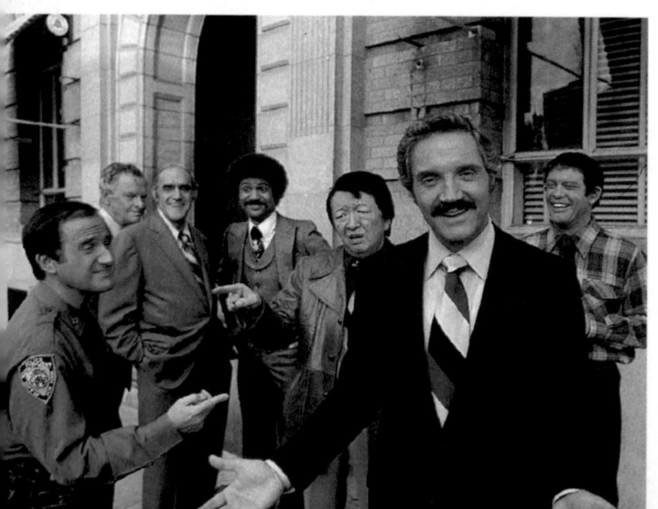

TAXI

LOUIE DROVE 'EM CRAZY, ALEX KEPT 'EM SANE: THESE BIG-APPLE CABBIES WERE ALWAYS GETTIN' IGGY WITH IT

JUST THE FACTS

BARNEY MILLER

YEARS ON AIR
1975–82

TOP NIELSEN CHARTING
16th (1978–79)

EMMYS WON
3

ORIGINAL TITLE
The Life and Times of Capt. Barney Miller (pilot)

SONG
The bass riff opening the show was written by folk legend Ramblin' Jack Elliott with Allyn Ferguson.

LOCKED DOWN
ABC didn't want to pick up *Miller* but finally said yes to snare director John Rich, who'd worked on *All In the Family*.

POSITIVE ID
After a previous show by producer Danny Arnold was considered "too ethnic," he named his new, still-Jewish character the less-Semitic "Miller."

LIGHT TOUCH
Though Arnold wanted to shoot on film, ABC insisted on tape to save money–but the producer still created filmic tones using special techniques.

WHAT DID THEY KNOW?
Linden tested "dull" in ABC's initial research.

SPIN-OFFS
Fish (1977–78)

TAXI

YEARS ON AIR
1978–83

TOP NIELSEN CHARTING
8th (1978–79)

EMMYS WON
18; 3 for Outstanding Comedy Series

ORIGINAL CONCEPT
Taxi was inspired by a *New York* magazine article about the drivers of Manhattan's Dover Cab Co., many of whom were aspiring actors and writers.

TESTOSTERONE FACTOR
After doing series about women (*The Mary Tyler Moore Show, Rhoda, Phyllis*), producer Ed. Weinberger wanted to do *Taxi* because "it was about guys."

THE METER'S RUNNING
After ABC canceled *Taxi* in '82, hit-hungry NBC bought it, then dropped it after one season.

ROAD RAGE
"You should put it back on the air," kvetched Hirsch in an Emmy acceptance speech after *Taxi* had been canceled.

CAST NOTES
Danny DeVito married his on- (and off-) screen girlfriend, Rhea Perlman.

THE BEAUTY OF A GREAT SITCOM ensemble is that even the lesser talents among the group can rise to the level of the material. After *Taxi* went off the air in 1983, various cast members drove off in vastly different directions: One became a comedy legend (Andy Kaufman, who died of cancer in 1984), one became a big movie star and director (Danny DeVito, ironically the most diminutive of the actors), another became a pop-cultural punching bag (Tony Danza, who starred in a series of limp family sitcoms), and yet another faded into oblivion (Jeff Conaway, whose *Taxi* role as a struggling actor now seems all too apt). ✦ Yet during their years of service at New York City's Sunshine Cab Co., every character contributed invaluably to the sitcom's wearily humane spirit. Judd Hirsch was the nominal lead as Übermensch cabbie Alex Rieger, but *Taxi* was not a star vehicle. The comic fuel was provided by the combustible combination of personalities inside the garage—a walking Napoleon complex (DeVito's dispatcher, Louie DePalma); an innocent immigrant (Kaufman's grease monkey, Latka Gravas); a mind-blown ex-hippie (Christopher Lloyd's "Reverend" Jim "Iggy" Ignatowski); and a drop-dead redhead (Marilu Henner's Elaine Nardo). ✦ Much credit must go to executive producer James L. Brooks and director James Burrows, who infused *Taxi* with the same workplace-as-dysfunctional-family feeling they helped create on *The Mary Tyler Moore Show*. And in doing so, they took viewers on a five-year ride as fun filled and surprising as a real taxi trip around Manhattan. —BF

JUST THE FACTS

EVERYBODY LOVES RAYMOND

YEARS ON AIR 1996–present

TOP NIELSEN CHARTING 33rd (1997–98)

EMMYS WON None

HOW IT BEGAN After being bumped twice, Romano appeared on David Letterman's show in 1995 but couldn't tell whether the inscrutable host loved or hated him. A few days later, Letterman's production company called to propose building a new sitcom around Romano.

ART IMITATES LIFE Like the character he plays, Romano grew up in Queens, N.Y., and lived at home until he married. He also has a brother who's a cop.

A HARD-EARNED LOVE The series placed at the bottom of the top 100 shows in its first season.

WHAT DID THEY KNOW? Martha Stewart, of all people, criticized Romano's humor for being "too tame." The star said it felt "like getting a punch from Mr. Rogers."

BEWITCHED

YEARS ON AIR 1964–72

TOP NIELSEN CHARTING 2nd (1964–65)

EMMYS WON 3

MAJOR MOMENT It was the biggest hit produced by ABC up to that time; until 1977, it was ABC's highest-rated prime-time half-hour show ever

MAID TO ORDER After Alice Ghostly wowed producers playing ditzy mortal maid Naomi, she was brought in to play ditzy witch Esmerelda

ORIGINAL CASTING Tammy Grimes (Samantha), Richard Crenna (Darrin)

BEWITCHING CAMEOS Raquel Welch (as a stewardess), Maureen McCormick (as a little witch), Richard Dreyfuss (as a warlock)

REPLACEMENT PARTS In 1969, when Dick Sargent replaced Dick York as Darrin, no one, least of all Samantha, seemed to notice.

SPIN-OFFS *Tabitha* (1977–78), starring Lisa Hartman as a grown-up Tabitha Stephens

EVERYBODY LOVES RAYMOND

THIS RELATIVE NEWCOMER TO THE FAMILY FUNNY BUSINESS STARTS A NEW TRADITION BY BEING BOTH SWEET AND TART

WHY DID WE INCLUDE THIS RELATIVE ROOKIE in the pantheon of great TV shows? Because with its mixture of timelessly witty writing and superbly unselfish ensemble acting, *Raymond* is a ready-made classic. "I'm doing the show for CBS, but in the back of my mind, I'm doing it for Nick at Nite," admits creator Phil Rosenthal. "I want it to last forever." ✦ So far, so good. Working with Rosenthal, cowriter-star Ray Romano took two seemingly dead-tired genres—the family comedy and the stand-up vehicle—and pumped fresh life into them. Closely modeled on his own life, Romano's show casts him as a sportswriter who lives on Long Island with his wife (Patricia Heaton) and three children (Madylin, Sullivan, and Sawyer Sweeten)—and right across the street from his pushy parents (Doris Roberts and Peter Boyle) and divorced-cop brother (Brad Garrett). Sounds like a standard sitcom setup, right? ✦ Wrong. What sets *Raymond* apart is the complexity of its characters. The interplay among the relatives is as acutely observed as that of any Eugene O'Neill play, and the scripts are laced with one-liners worthy of early Woody Allen (Raymond on his life's ambition: "I always thought that I wanted to write the Great American Novel. But then I remembered, I don't even want to *read* the Great American Novel"). As smartly written as *Seinfeld*, as finely acted as *Frasier*, *Raymond* deserves everybody's love. And even if it's never a huge hit on CBS, well, there's always Nick at Nite. —BF/PHOTOGRAPH BY JIM WRIGHT

BEWITCHED

A TWITCHY WITCH PUT A SEXY TWIST ON SUBURBAN LIFE

ELIZABETH MONTGOMERY DIDN'T WANT TO WORK in TV. The daughter of Hollywood actor Robert Montgomery, who had hosted an anthology show on NBC for seven years, she had seen how television-production schedules ate up one's life. She did, however, want to work with her new husband, producer William Asher, and when his concept about a suburban witch caught on with ABC, she signed up for the lead role of Samantha Stephens—filming the first shows less than a month after giving birth to the couple's first child. ✦ That hints at the hard work put into a show that only looked like goofy fluff. *Bewitched* retooled movies like 1942's *I Married a Witch* and 1958's *Bell, Book and Candle* for the complacent *Leave It to Beaver* generation, but the show, as knowing as its star, also tracked the paradoxes of its era. Peek behind those vanishing coffee tables and Darrin's miraculously saved ad accounts and you'll see a series that was explicitly about the dilemma of the modern housewife, possessed of hidden powers yet unable to use them for much more than vacuuming the living room. ✦ The split turned even more baroque: On Jan. 13, 1966, when Samantha settled further into asexual domesticity by giving birth to baby Tabitha, her hot-to-trot "twin cousin"—played by "Pandora Spocks"—was introduced in the very same episode. It didn't matter that two different actors (Dicks York and Sargent) played Darrin over the course of the series' eight-year run: He, mother Endora (Agnes Moorehead), and all those crazed relatives were intended as glorious cartoons. But sensible Sam earned our laughs and empathy, twitching her nose and watching the world change around her. —TD

JUST THE FACTS

THE DICK VAN DYKE SHOW

YEARS ON AIR
1961–66

TOP NIELSEN CHARTING
3rd (1963–64); never out of top 20

EMMYS WON
15

ORIGINAL TITLE
Head of the Family (pilot)

ORIGINAL CASTING
In the pilot, Carl Reiner played Rob and Barbara Britton was his wife. The original choice for Laura was Eileen Brennan; but Moore (previously a dancing elf in Hotpoint Appliances stove ads) got the job after being recommended by Danny Thomas, who'd auditioned her as his daughter on *Make Room for Daddy.*

OTTOMAN EMPIRE
Earle Hagen, who wrote the show's trippy (literally) opening instrumental tune, also wrote *The Andy Griffith Show*'s theme.

WE BOW BEFORE HIM
Van Dyke's show is so revered he was named the unofficial "chairman" of Nick at Nite in 1992.

FRIENDS

YEARS ON AIR
1994–present

TOP NIELSEN CHARTING
3rd (1995–96)

EMMYS WON
1

ORIGINAL TITLE
Friends Like Us (also considered: *Insomnia Cafe, Six of One, Across the Hall*)

WE KNEW HER WHEN
Courteney Cox's big break came in 1984, when director Brian DePalma cast her as the girl Bruce Springsteen "spontaneously" pulls out of the audience to frolic on stage in the video of "Dancing in the Dark."

ROLE REVERSAL
Cox was originally considered for the role of Rachel, which went to Jennifer Aniston. Aniston had read for the part of Monica, which went to Cox.

PERRY INTERESTING
As a teenager in Canada, Matthew Perry was a nationally ranked junior tennis player and considered turning pro before opting for an acting career instead.

IT COULD BE ARGUED THAT the modern sitcom began with *The Dick Van Dyke Show*: The series gave equal time to its main character's work life and family life (in the days of *Leave It to Beaver* and *Father Knows Best*, we rarely saw Dad at the office). It allowed a wife to be just as funny as her husband (which had occurred only in extraordinary instances, like *I Love Lucy*). And it dared to satirize the TV industry decades before *The Larry Sanders Show.* ✦ Van Dyke brought a dancer's grace to the role of Rob Petrie, head writer of *The Alan Brady Show* (in a nice twist, the temperamental titular star was played by creator Carl Reiner). As the winsome Laura, Mary Tyler Moore was the sexiest housewife in small-screen history, so fetching that she was allowed to wear her trademark butt-hugging capri pants in only one scene per episode. Their young son, Ritchie (Larry Mathews), played a minor role, but that was just fine; there were plenty of juvenile antics from Rob's cowriters, husband-hunting Sally Rogers (Rose Marie) and perpetual borscht belt wisecracker Buddy Sorrell (Morey Amsterdam), who delighted in insulting producer (and Alan Brady brother-in-law) Mel Cooley (Richard Deacon). ✦ Classic episodes abounded. Remember when Laura gets her toe stuck in the bathtub faucet? When Rob dreams about ever-present walnuts and an alien with no thumbs that looks like Danny Thomas? In a true mark of class, *The Dick Van Dyke Show* went out riding high—still in the top 20 and with four straight Outstanding Comedy Emmys. In doing so, it upheld that cardinal rule of showbiz: Always leave 'em wanting more. —BF/PHOTOGRAPH BY ALLAN GRANT

A SITCOM ABOUT A TV WRITER? A SHOW THAT LAUGHED AT THE WORKPLACE AND AT HOME LIFE? 'DVD' WAS A REAL COMEDY TRIP.

THE DICK VAN DYKE SHOW

FIRST, LET'S KEEP THIS IN MIND: THE THEME song was not their fault. Neither was the hairstyle craze, the relentless media hype, nor the sadly inadequate stream of copycat sitcoms that crammed the networks in the fall of 1995, a year after *Friends* debuted on NBC. What this good-looking sextet should take responsibility for is forging a rare TV phenomenon: an honest-to-goodness ensemble comedy that perfectly captured the mood of its decade. ✦ How'd they do it? Simple, really. Take a random sampling of six twenty-somethings, add some lively banter, flavor with pop-culture references ("I'd much rather be Mr. Peanut than Mr. Salty!"), throw in a pinch of romance, then steep on a coffee-shop couch. Dismissed at first as a Gen-X *Seinfeld*, *Friends* is actually about something: the makeshift (and often malfunctioning) family we find upon moving into the real world after college. This one featured Monica (Courteney Cox), the neurotic mother hen; Phoebe (Lisa Kudrow), the New Age massage therapist; Rachel (Jennifer Aniston), the rich girl struggling to find an identity; Ross (David Schwimmer), the poor schmuck dumped by his wife for a woman; Chandler (Matthew Perry), the wisecracking clown; and Joey (Matt LeBlanc), the dim-witted ladies' man. The six relatively unknown actors became a house blend of post-slacker comedy by never allowing one character's sweetness or another's bitterness to overwhelm the brew. ✦ That may not sound impressive, but portraying a group of pals pursuing life's idle pleasures—spying on an ugly naked neighbor, playing Twister, staging a "boyfriend bonfire"—without making it look contrived and cloying is a rare feat in the punchline-or-bust sitcom world. In other words, these guys are the best friends television ever had.

—KRISTEN BALDWIN/PHOTOGRAPH BY ANDREW ECCLES

GEN-XERS' FAVORITE SIX-PACK

FRIENDS

JUST THE FACTS

THE JACK BENNY SHOW

YEARS ON AIR 1950–65

TOP NIELSEN CHARTING 5th (1955–56)

EMMYS WON 7

ART DOESN'T IMITATE LIFE
Benny, who feigned being a bad fiddler, had actually begun his career as a vaudeville violinist and owned a Stradivarius. Contrary to his cheapskate persona, he was a generous philanthropist.

INSTINCTIVE COMEDY
Asked why he put three fingers to his cheek during his trademark stare, Benny answered, "Because three fingers are funnier than four."

A STARSTRUCK KID
After Johnny Carson took over *The Tonight Show*, Benny called, offering to fill in if any guests canceled. Carson, who idolized Benny, was strangely unresponsive. Benny later learned that Carson had assumed the call was a prank.

AIN'T NO SUNSHINE
Terminal cancer prevented Benny from starring in *The Sunshine Boys.* So best friend George Burns took the part–and won an Oscar.

THE BOB NEWHART SHOW

YEARS ON AIR 1972–78

TOP NIELSEN CHARTING 12th (1973–74)

EMMYS WON 0

BEACH MUSIC
David Davis and Lorenzo Music wrote the pilot during a four-day writing marathon at the beach in Santa Barbara, Calif.

ORIGINAL CONCEPT
Bob, a conservative Freudian therapist, shares an office with Jerry, a freewheeling Jungian therapist. After the pilot was filmed, CBS decided two psychologists was one too many; Jerry became an orthodontist.

HEAD GAMES?
The number on Bob's office sometimes read "751," sometimes "715."

THAT DEADPAN EXPRESSION IS REAL
Newhart was once an accountant.

BOB, ARE YOU TIRED?
Bob and Emily climbing into their king-size bed was the death knell for the long-held network conceit that married couples slept separately.

THE GREAT DEADPAN CHEAPSKATE, Jack Benny parlayed a successful career in vaudeville and radio, and a middling one in film (his persona-defining role in Ernst Lubitsch's 1942 *To Be or Not to Be* was probably his cinematic high point), to arrive at this pre-postmodern CBS sitcom, in which he played a character not unlike himself, a successful comedian surrounded by friends and oddballs. Benny's quiet, self-effacing style—a comedy of long, thoughtful poses followed by fey exasperation (he turned the expostulation "Well!" into a catch-phrase)—wouldn't have seemed well suited to the harsh glare and speedy pace of television, but the public took to it just fine (in fact, his show lasted a remarkable 15 years). ✦ Benny—whose top-notch guest list included such big stars as Frank Sinatra and Marilyn Monroe—also surrounded himself with a strong roster of supporting players, chief among them Eddie "Rochester" Anderson, who played

JACK BENNY SHOW

his valet. This African-American caricature was racist at its core, but Anderson himself was a brilliant performer, using his gravelly voice and wily charm to beguile audiences and outwit Benny in most of their paper-thin plots. From radio, Benny also brought with him the perennially callow singer Dennis Day and Mel Blanc (far left), who would become legendary as the voice for every major Warner Bros. cartoon character from Bugs Bunny to Daffy Duck. With all of them, Benny reacted to their broad antics with subdued surprise and sly mockery; it is a comic style that has since been an influence on everyone from Bob Newhart to David Letterman. —KT

THE MISERLY FIDDLER WAS A MASTER AT PLAYING THE AUDIENCE FOR LAUGHS

WHEN CBS ASKED BOB NEWHART to star as a shrink, the stand-up comic had two reservations. First, he wanted to play a psychologist, not a psychiatrist. "A psychologist treats people who are overweight or fear flying," he explains. "I didn't want to make fun of schizophrenics and manic-depressives." Second, he wasn't interested in having kids: "I didn't want to play 'Oh, look at the pickle Dad got into.' Then the kids straighten it all out and say, 'Dad, we love you, but boy, you're stupid.' " ✦ Smart decisions both. As Bob Hartley, the married-without-children Chicago psychologist, Newhart found the perfect vehicle for his ultra-low-key humor. The finest reactor in TV history, Newhart was surrounded by lunatics, some of them patients (Jack Riley's misanthropic Mr. Carlin), others coworkers (Marcia Wallace's man-chasing Carol Kester) and neighbors (Bill Daily's clueless Howard Borden). His marriage to Suzanne Pleshette's Emily was so indelible, she reappeared in the surreal finale of Bob's next sitcom, *Newhart*. ✦ In the middle of this madness stood Bob, an Everyman with whom everyone could identify. "Wives say, 'Oh, that's my husband,' husbands say, 'Oh, that's what I do,' and the younger generation says, 'That's my dad,' " Newhart explains of his enduring appeal. Of course, there is *one* other factor: " 'Hi, Bob' had something to do with [it]," he admits of the drinking game (chug when you hear that phrase!). "But I don't want to go down in history for that." No problem there. —BF

THE BOB NEWHART SHOW

HIS LOW-KEY HUMOR MADE HIM OUR FAVORITE SESSION MAN

JUST THE FACTS

THE COSBY SHOW

YEARS ON AIR 1984–92

TOP NIELSEN CHARTING 1st (1985–88)

EMMYS WON 6

A DOCTOR IN THE HOUSE Cosby used the series to showcase child-rearing theories he formed while earning his doctoral degree in education.

HOW IT ALL BEGAN NBC's Brandon Tartikoff saw one of Cosby's *Tonight Show* monologues about life with his children and thought it would make a good sitcom.

TURNAROUND The year before its debut, only one of the top 13 shows was a sitcom; three years later, 7 of the top 10 were sitcoms.

GO FIGURE *Cosby* was a hit in segregated South Africa.

LAUGH RIOT The final episode aired on April 30, 1992—the second night of the L.A. riots. Mayor Tom Bradley pleaded with Los Angelenos to "observe the curfew and watch *The Cosby Show*." Many didn't.

MONTY PYTHON'S FLYING CIRCUS

YEARS ON AIR 1969–74 (BBC)

TOP NIELSEN CHARTING Not available

EMMYS WON 0

HOW THEY MET Various Python members had worked together on a series of British TV shows, including *That Was the Week That Was*, *The Frost Report*, and *Do Not Adjust Your Set*.

UPPER-CLASS CLOWNS Most of the troupe were educated at Oxford (Michael Palin and Terry Jones) and Cambridge (Graham Chapman, John Cleese, and Eric Idle).

THAT POMPOUS THEME SONG It's not British, actually; it's John Philip Sousa's "The Liberty Bell," and it was chosen in part because it was in the public domain and thus didn't require the payment of copyright fees.

LEGITIMACY Several *Python* catchphrases have found their way into *Bartlett's Familiar Quotations*, including "This is an ex-parrot!" and the lyrics to "The Lumberjack Song."

THE COSBY SHOW

WHEN THE MUST-SEE HUXTABLES INVITED US INTO THEIR HAPPY HOME, THEY ASKED US TO CHECK OUR STEREOTYPES AT THE DOOR

JUST FOR THE RECORD, we owe Thursday night as we know it to William H. Cosby Jr., Ed.D. Before *The Cosby Show*, a sweet-hearted look at the earnestly upper-middle-class Huxtable clan, NBC was in third place in the ratings and the fifth night of the week was simply the day before Friday. But *The Cosby Show*'s ascension made for must-see TV years before that overused promo line began assaulting the national psyche. ✦ At a time when television was dominated by car chases, gunplay, and miniskirts, and sitcoms were considered passé, *The Cosby Show* was something of a return to grace. Created by Cosby, Ed. Weinberger, and Michael Leeson, the show centered on Heathcliff and Clair Huxtable (Phylicia Rashad), a blessedly sane doctor-and-lawyer married couple, and their five precocious children. And that was that. Just life with the Huxtables. Period. "You have to remember how different a show we were proposing," executive producer Tom Werner told TIME magazine in 1987. "Instead of getting laughs from arguments and conflicts...we were going for subtler humor." Life lessons like the death of a goldfish, bad grades, even the borrowing of Dad's car all served as the bedrock for *Cosby*'s particular brand of smirking, my-way-or-the-subway merriment. And that subtler approach worked. For four consecutive seasons, Cosby was rated No. 1–a record equaled only by *Gunsmoke* and bested only by *All in the Family*. Wisely, NBC built on the *Cosby* foundation, and–with shows like *Cheers, L.A. Law*, and, ultimately, *Seinfeld*–became America's No. 1 network. ✦ But for me, *The Cosby Show* was special for another, vastly more important reason. I was 13 when the show premiered, and for the first time, I saw me on the TV screen: I saw a middle-class black family just being, doing what families do, free of the street drama and ghetto stereotypes that burdened programs like *Good Times* and *Sanford and Son*. For the first time, I–and the rest of the world–was invited into the lives of Americans who just happened to also be African. —MARC BERNARDIN

TALK ABOUT THE FULL MONTY: THIS SEXTET EXPOSED US TO A NEW THEATER OF THE ABSURD

IT WAS 1969, and the staid British Broadcasting Corporation fancied itself ready for something different. Something *completely* different. How could the BBC have known what it was getting itself into? Never before, and never since, has there been anything remotely like that free-form amalgam of parody, satire, music, drag, animation, and unabated silliness that was *Monty Python's Flying Circus*. ✦ Starring a six-member troupe that conjoined august Oxbridge theatrical talent with one way-out American, *Python*, which aired first in Britain before arriving Stateside on PBS in 1974, twitted the starchy drawing-room manners to which much of England clung in the '60s and '70s (quite literally: See "The Upper-Class Twit of the Year Contest"). Some of the best material spoofed the BBC's standard repertoire of sepulchral-toned news programs and droning nature shows ("The Larch. The...Larch") Other skits tweaked historical events and figures (who would have expected the Spanish Inquisition, let alone Oscar Wilde, to show up in sketch comedy?). And a good portion was total non-sequitur absurdity. (A fish-slapping dance?) ✦ But every *Python* fan–and they're an obsessive bunch–has his or her own pet bits. Terry Jones' nude organist, Eric Idle's insinuating pest ("nudge, nudge"), Michael Palin's singing lumberjack, and John Cleese's masterfully deadpan Mr. Teabags from the Ministry of Silly Walks all left indelible impressions (Cleese quit before the final year, moving on to the hilarious hotel farce *Fawlty Towers*). None of this could have possibly held together were it not for the Yankee Terry Gilliam's surreal, lumpy, often rather icky cartoons. ✦ Of course, some thought *Python* went a bit too far into the Department of Grotesque (one cannibalism-themed episode, for example, was never fully rebroadcast in England). But for those who delighted in playing spot the loony–with six of them, it was hard to lose–*Python* could never have gone far enough. —ALEXANDRA JACOBS

FAMILY TIES

GREED WAS GOOD—AND VERY FUNNY—THANKS TO THE SLY APPEAL OF MICHAEL J. FOX

WHEN NBC ENTERTAINMENT president Brandon Tartikoff first saw the pilot for *Family Ties* in 1982, he loved everything about it—except Michael J. Fox. Thankfully, creator Gary David Goldberg fought for the unknown Canadian actor he had chosen for the role of young Republican Alex P. Keaton. And it's a good thing he did: After struggling in the ratings, *Family Ties* got a big boost in 1985 when Fox appeared in a little film called *Back to the Future*. ✦ But it wasn't just Fox's movie stardom that made *Family Ties* a hit. It was his winning personality. Fox took a potentially obnoxious character and made him seem charmingly vulnerable. Soon, a sitcom that had started out being about ex-hippie parents (Meredith Baxter-Birney and Michael Gross) and their Reaganite offspring (Fox, Justine Bateman, and Tina Yothers) became a showcase for Fox's impeccable comic timing. ✦ Not that it was a one-man show. In addition to the Keaton clan, there was a stellar backup cast, including Tom Hanks (who was on the verge of making his big *Splash*) as the kids' no-account uncle Ned; Marc Price as Alex's gloriously doofy pal, Skippy; and Tracy Pollan (Fox's future wife) and Courteney Cox (cutting her sitcom teeth nearly a decade before *Friends*) as two of Alex's girlfriends. ✦ Along with *The Cosby Show* (which it followed on Thursday nights from 1984 to '87), *Family Ties* made '80s materialism seem appealingly all-American. More important, it introduced a star perfectly suited to the small screen, which Fox still demonstrates as the Alex P. Keatonesque deputy mayor on ABC's *Spin City*. —BF

MARY HARTMAN, MARY HARTMAN

LEAR'S SPOOF OF TV AT ITS WORST PROVED TO BE TV AT ITS WACKIEST

NORMAN LEAR HAD ALWAYS BEEN a magnet for controversy. Having unleashed *All in the Family* on the viewing public in 1971, he soon after proposed another groundbreaking concept: a soap opera parody that would premiere with a mass murder, an octogenarian flasher, and an impotent husband. Thanks, but no thanks, all three networks said. So Lear took another bold step—he sold the series in first-run syndication and created a virtual ad hoc network all his own. ✦The 1976 show, set in the fictional town of Fernwood, Ohio, centered on Mary Hartman (Louise Lasser), a pigtailed, somewhat obtuse suburban housewife addicted to TV commercials, whose biggest concern in life was the "waxy yellow buildup" on her kitchen floor. Lampooning both Americans' obsession with television and the medium itself, the program featured offbeat characters (an 8-year-old evangelist) and kinky plot twists (Mary's father had plastic surgery to look like Tab Hunter—and then was played by Tab Hunter). Things only got crazier as time went on: In one episode, a neighbor drowned in a bowl of soup; in another, a TV celebrity was impaled on an aluminum Christmas tree. ✦ The first-season finale said a lot about Lear's opinion of television. In it, Mary has a nervous breakdown and ends up (by season two) in an insane asylum—only to discover that her fellow inmates are part of the "Nielsen family," a group chosen to represent national TV viewing habits. How would that imaginary group have described *Mary Hartman, Mary Hartman*? Hilarious, hilarious. —TOM SOTER

S

AIR 1982–89

EN CHARTING 2nd 986–87)

N 5

CASTING Matthew as Alex P. Keaton (he

S LIFE The birth of w during the 1984–85 ncided with Baxter- l-life pregnancy. (She o twins.)

CAMEOS President Ronald Reagan pronounced *Family Ties* his favorite series, and there was talk of his appearing in an episode; it never panned out.

LIFE IMITATES ART Goldberg took the series premise–a former flower child settled in suburbia–from his own life, but he became so rich from *Family Ties* that Grant Tinker once reportedly chided him, "It's not that you sold out; it's that you sold out so completely."

MARY HARTMAN, MARY HARTMAN

YEARS ON AIR 1976–77

TOP NIELSEN CHARTING Never ranked in top 25.

EMMYS WON 3

THE PRICE OF SUCCESS Even as the show was scoring a critical and ratings coup, it was losing almost $50,000 each week, because of the low fees paid by local stations.

THE PRICE OF TALENT Lasser turned down the lead several times before finally agreeing to come aboard–for $5,000 a week and the freedom to leave after one year, which she did.

COMING TOGETHER To achieve the half-parody/half-genuine feel of the show, Lear paired writers with contrasting backgrounds, such as Ann Marcus (who had been head writer for the soap *Search for Tomorrow*) and Gail Parent (who penned the "As the Stomach Turns" soap spoof on *The Carol Burnett Show*).

THE BEST GAME SHOWS OF ALL TIME

GAME SHOWS ARE THE RODNEY DANGERFIELD OF TV GENRES—THEY GET NO RESPECT FROM SNOOTY CRITICS. STILL, THEY'RE JUST TOO ENTERTAINING TO GO AWAY. THEY'VE SURVIVED EVERYTHING FROM A HUGE SCANDAL IN THE '50S TO JENNY McCARTHY IN THE '90S. LONG LIVE TURTLE WAX AND SOUND BOOTHS! HEREWITH, A.J. JACOBS' LOOK AT THE BEST OF THE BUNCH:

Jeopardy!

1 JEOPARDY! The category is great game shows. Created by Merv Griffin, it has been featured in such flicks as *White Men Can't Jump*, and it actually requires some gray matter. What is...well, you know. Since its 1964 debut, *Jeopardy!* has become America's brainteaser of choice, as addictive as a potent potable. First hosted by the genial Art Fleming, and now by stern headmaster Alex Trebek, the daily quiz show has given us the questions to more than 200,000 answers since returning to the air in 1984. It has truly earned that exclamation point.

---

2 WHEEL OF FORTUNE And now for the anti-*Jeopardy!*: simple, silly, and completely mindless. Based on the childhood game hangman, *Wheel* shows three contestants (the dimmer the better) spinning a wheel, clapping too much, buying vowels, and trying to figure out a name or phrase. Created by the prolific Griffin in 1975, the show initially featured Chuck Woolery and Susan Stafford. It now airs in 31 countries (53 if you include its 22 foreign clones) and teams Pat Sajak's amiable condescension with Vanna White's flawless, Pavlovian letter-turning.

---

3 THE GONG SHOW Never has TV featured so many hilariously untalented people in one place. In this Chuck Barris-created amateur half hour (1976-80), viewers were subjected to eardrum-splitting renditions of "Feelings," jokes from The Unknown Comic, a woman who whistled through her nose, and—GONG!—we'll channel the spirit of celeb judge Jamie Farr and spare you the rest. Except to add that the 1980 *Gong Show Movie*—consisting of a behind-the-scenes look at the program—was quickly gonged right out of theaters.

---

4 WHAT'S MY LINE? Imagine Susan Sontag and Henry Louis Gates Jr. on a game show today. Not gonna happen. But this 1950-67 classic—the longest-running game show in prime-time history—featured delightfully witty highbrow panelists: Woody Allen, publisher Bennett Cerf, columnist Dorothy Kilgallen, and talk-meister Steve Allen, who came up with the show's signature question, "Is it bigger than a bread box?" The game's point: Guess the occupation of a mystery

Family Feud

guest—who could be anyone from a hatcheck girl to a movie star. But the real draw was all that Algonquin-round-table banter.

5 HOLLYWOOD SQUARES From sublime panelists to ridiculous ones: In this schlock-fest (it had an impressive run from 1966 to '81 and then reappeared intermittently in the '80s), nine celebs sat inside a three-story ticktacktoe board and parried questions with wacky ad-libs (which turned out to be scripted). And what gloriously B-list celebs they were: Waylon Flowers and his puppet Madame, Shadoe Stevens, and that most famous wiseacre center square, Paul Lynde. (Lynde was once asked, "Who was known during World War II as Old Blood and Guts?" His reply: "Barbara Stanwyck.") A new version, scheduled to debut in October, will feature Whoopi Goldberg. And the word *whoopee* brings us to...

6 THE NEWLYWED GAME It was a marriage made in TV heaven: freshly wed couples revealing bedroom habits and a late-'60s audience hungry for titillation. Hosted by the smirking Bob Eubanks (and, briefly in '89, by comic Paul Rodriguez), the show won the double entendre sweepstakes (runners-up *Match Game* and *The Dating Game*, please enjoy some lovely parting gifts). Mr. and Mrs. Contestant would try to match answers to such naughty questions as "Where's the strangest place you've ever made whoopee?" (Sadly, no one ever gave the legendary answer involving a posterior body part.) A new, fairly cheese-free '90s version wasn't nearly as much fun.

7 THE PRICE IS RIGHT Capitalist porn at its purest, *Price* makes no pretense about European history or head-scratching word puzzles. It's all about prizes—lots of fabulous prizes—and overexcited contestants who "come on down!" to guess their market value. Dreamed up by game-show titans Mark Goodson and Bill Todman, *Price* has tempted us with Buick Skylarks and trips to Bermuda for an astounding four decades—and still does, with host Bob Barker and his team of curvaceous assistants presiding over this priceless bit of television.

8 LET'S MAKE A DEAL Before *Jerry Springer*, this was TV's prime place to humiliate yourself. Monty, look at me! I'm a chicken! I'm corn on the cob! Audience members squeezed themselves into wacky costumes hoping to get chosen by even-tempered host Monty Hall. If they did, they gambled small prizes for whatever was hidden behind Door No. 1, 2, or 3. Would it be an exotic trip, or—wah, wah!—a rotten apple? Whichever, it was a good deal for viewers.

9 YOU BET YOUR LIFE The secret word is *Groucho*. This 1950-61 quizzer was hosted by the great cigar-chomping Marx Brother himself—this time with a real mustache instead of the black paint smear he wore in the movies. The former vaudevillian's absurd, extended interviews with contestants made this show more fun than a day at the races. And more monkey business came at the end: Losers won consolation prizes by answering such doozies as "Who's buried in Grant's Tomb?" Later versions with Buddy Hackett and Bill Cosby fizzled.

10 FAMILY FEUD Name the smarmiest talk-show host ever. Survey *says*: Richard Dawson. With his sloppy kisses and lascivious patter, the former *Hogan's Heroes* star made for can't-miss TV (Dawson had two reigns: 1976-85 and 1994-95; the tamer Ray Combs hosted a 1988-94 version). The contest itself was almost as amusing. Feudal lord Dawson would ask a question like "Name the most popular vacation spot on the East Coast." Two battling clans would then try to match answers with 100 people surveyed. You had to love the familial support: No matter how dumb Junior's response, his relatives always shouted a supportive "Good answer!"

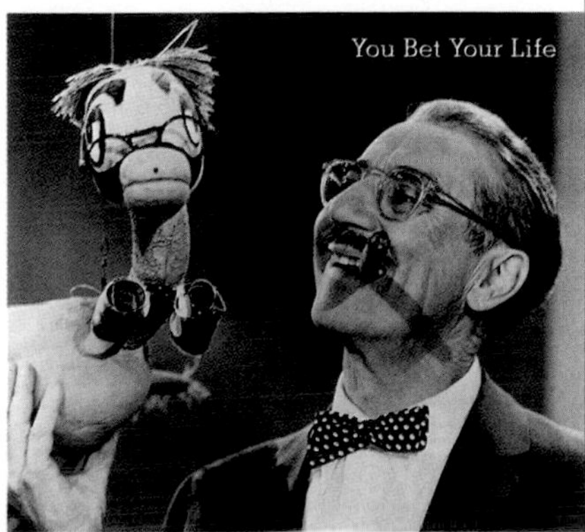
You Bet Your Life

INTERARMS
ALEXANDRIA VIRGINIA
AD76624

DRAMAS

TELEVISION HAS ACHED FOR RESPECT FROM THE VERY BEGINNING, and nothing grants respect like drama. On Sept. 11, 1928, just five years after the first test images had flickered on a laboratory receiver, an adaptation of J. Hartley Manners' one-act play *The Queen's Messenger* was broadcast over fledgling WGY in Schenectady, N.Y. *The New York Times* gave it a qualified rave, noting that "the pictures are about the size of a postal card and are sometimes blurred and confused." ✦ The visuals have improved since then, but after a long dalliance with clarity, modern TV dramas are once again looking rather "blurred and confused"—and that's for the better. The time-honored genres still hold, of course: Police shows focus on the chase, private-eye shows on the mystery, lawyer shows on the process. Westerns are about the tension between civilization and anarchy, doctor shows are compressed inquisitions into life and death, and "life dramas" as varied as *The Waltons, Peyton Place,* and *thirtysomething* look at the pressures of a self-contained community. But today the doctors of *ER* and the cops of *NYPD Blue* wrestle with ethical dilemmas that make Hollywood movies look cartoonish by comparison, detective shows flirt with deconstructive camp, and "life dramas" have found fertile new teenage territory when not turning downright surreal (*Twin Peaks*). ✦ At the dawn of the '60s, though, only *Alfred Hitchcock Presents* and the ahead-of-its time *Maverick* (featuring James Garner's turn-and-run Western hero) knowingly winked at the audience. The rest of the dramatic schedule was filled with honest medics like Dr. Kildare, stalwart lawyers like Perry Mason, the uncomplicated cowpokes of *Bonanza* and *Rawhide*—and *The Fugitive*'s unjustly accused, terribly serious Richard Kimble. As the decade progressed and the culture began entertaining doubts about itself, however, a certain archness began creeping into the on-air mix, starting with the espionage genre. *I Spy* and *The Avengers* aped the chic, cynical aplomb of the James Bond films; *Mission: Impossible* took Bond's high-tech plots and amped them until they were densely absurd. ✦ Then the gumshoes got ironic. During the '70s, Kojak sucked his lollipops, Columbo kept coming back for one last question, and Rockford stumbled through one case after another. Around this time, though, other dramatic genres started going straight again. *The Waltons* and *Little House on the Prairie* brought back the life drama with a graceful lack of irony, and, with *Roots*, the miniseries suddenly looked to be the epically serious format the medium had long been searching for. ✦ About the only holdouts from all this hipness were the cops, unless you count *Dragnet*, which had always been so woodenly straight that it played as parody. But that changed too, with the advent of *Hill Street Blues* in 1981, and with the shows that followed in its moody wake: *Cagney & Lacey, St. Elsewhere, L.A. Law, ER*. Where TV had once insisted that these professionals were society's guardian angels, now we saw that they were *us*, with all the attendant and beguiling complexities. As commentator Steven D. Stark says about *ER* in his book *Glued to the Set*, "The doctors themselves—self-absorbed baby boomers—had to deal with the existential problems that [Marcus] Welby had once detected in his patients." ✦ About the only thing that *hasn't* changed in 50 years of TV drama is that we're still watching shows about cops, doctors, lawyers, and detectives. But as that sage programmer Fred Silverman once noted of TV's heroes, "What are they going to be? Architects? What will *happen* to them?" —TY BURR

PHOTOGRAPH BY NOLA LÓPEZ

THE FUGITIVE

THE GREAT ESCAPE: FOR FOUR YEARS, WE WERE CAPTURED BY THIS MAN ON THE RUN

IN 1963, WHEN ABC AIRED A SERIES about a wrongly convicted doctor who goes on the lam to find his wife's real killer, it was, some claim, no coincidence: A federal judge had recently ordered that convicted Cleveland osteopath Sam Sheppard be granted a second trial in the killing of *his* wife, and the public's lurid fascination with the case was at a fever pitch. Did he or didn't he? ✦ When *The Fugitive* premiered that September, William Conrad's stentorian opening narration absolved viewers of any troubling moral ambiguity about *this* doctor's guilt: By assuring them that Dr. Richard Kimble was an innocent victim of "blind justice," Conrad set in motion the greatest cat-and-mouse game in TV history. For the next four years, the series' setting and supporting cast changed weekly, as Kimble (played with a brooding sexiness by David Janssen) improvised his way across the country, changing identities, hair color, jobs, and love interests. Always, the one-armed man he knew to be the killer was tantalizingly out of reach. And always, Kimble's dogged pursuer, Lieut. Philip Gerard, was a mere step behind. ✦ Finally, after multiple stab and gunshot wounds and too many illnesses to count, Janssen got tired of all that running and wanted out. But producer Quinn Martin didn't just let the series fade unresolved into oblivion; he created a true tie-up-the-loose-ends finale. In the Aug. 29, 1967, ender (the most-watched program in history up to that time), Kimble finally met up with his quarry atop a water tower, where the one-armed man confessed before being shot by Lieutenant Gerard and falling to his death below. The cat had caught his mouse at last. —MATTHEW MCCANN FENTON

THE FUGITIVE

YEARS ON AIR 1963–67

TOP NIELSEN CHARTING 5th (1964–65)

EMMYS WON 1

HOW IT ALL BEGAN Writer-producer Roy Huggins based his original idea on Victor Hugo's *Les Misérables.*

FINE-TUNING THE CONCEPT ABC execs worried that viewers would feel Dr. Kimble's only honorable alternative was to turn himself in. To address this, the producers came up with a scenario that explained why he couldn't (he was facing the death penalty) and absolved him of the moral stigma associated with fleeing the law (Kimble hadn't planned to run and didn't resort to violence to get away; a train wreck gave him the opportunity).

CAMEOS BY CENTRAL CHARACTERS Kimble's pursuer (Lieut. Philip Gerard, played by Barry Morse) and his quarry (the one-armed man, played by Bill Raisch) were rarely seen. Morse appeared in about one out of every four episodes; Raisch worked just four days during the first two years of production.

EQUAL OPPORTUNITY CASTING Raisch, who lost his arm in combat during World War II, also served as Burt Lancaster's regular stand-in.

GOING OUT WITH A BANG The second half of the two-part finale was, at the time, the highest-rated episode of any weekly program ever, and to this day has been bested only by the "Who Shot J.R.?" episode of *Dallas* and the finale of *M*A*S*H.*

LEGACY Imitators (*Run for Your Life*; *The Invaders*; *Run, Buddy, Run*) abounded but never amounted to much. The '90s prime-time drama *Quantum Leap* owed a great deal to *The Fugitive.* The one-armed man in *Twin Peaks* is an overt homage to the influence of the series.

JUST THE FACTS

JUST THE FACTS

MOONLIGHTING

YEARS ON AIR 1985–89

TOP NIELSEN CHARTING 9th (1986–87)

EMMYS WON 5

TYPECASTING The role of ex-fashion model Maddie was written with ex-fashion model Shepherd in mind.

BIG BREAK Willis was the last of 3,000 actors who auditioned for the lead.

PRODUCTION NOTES Elaborate scenarios and on-set tension led to delays that prevented *Moonlighting* from delivering 22 episodes during the 1985–86 season (ABC got 20 instead) and led to one episode being several minutes short. (Willis and Shepherd made up the time by talking to the camera.)

FAST TALKIN' The rapid-fire repartee between Willis and Shepherd made each script double the usual length for an hour-long series.

GENIUS ISN'T CHEAP The average weekly budget was $1.6 million, making it one of TV's priciest hour-long series.

THE AVENGERS

YEARS ON AIR 1966–69

TOP NIELSEN CHARTING Never cracked the top 35

EMMYS WON 0

ORIGINAL CONCEPT The series was created as an action-adventure show, with a gun-toting leading man. But Macnee (who had seen a number of friends shot during World War II) refused to carry a gun, opting for an umbrella.

WHAT'S IN A NAME? Emma Peel was christened for the demographic she was meant to attract: Male Appeal (or M Appeal).

A TIDY SUM *The Avengers* earned a fortune for Macnee, who had a 21 percent share of the profits.

AN UN-TIDY SUM Rigg earned less per episode than the show's makeup person.

NOBLE IDEAS Macnee claims descent from Robin Hood and Scottish king David VII.

SPIN-OFFS 1976's *The New Avengers*, with Macnee—and *Ab Fab*'s Joanna Lumley!

YOU KNEW IT THE MINUTE you saw him—the cocksure swagger, the barroom eyes, the quarterback smile. Bruce Willis was a Star, even if he was only the lead of ABC's crime-time detective dramedy *Moonlighting.* As too-hip-for-the-room private dick David Addison, Willis was like David Lee Roth with a badge; he sang, he limboed, he solved crimes, and, as time went on, he watched his hairline recede. The razor-sharp repartee that Willis shared with luminous costar Cybill Shepherd, as fleeced ex-cover girl Maddie Hayes, and the show's gleeful irreverence helped make it a *Thin Man* for the opulent '80s. ✦ Created by ex-*Remington Steele* writer Glenn Gordon Caron, *Moonlighting* virtually redefined screwball comedies for the postfeminist era. For almost five seasons, Maddie screamed at David. David howled back.

Maddie threw something. David ducked. And maybe they did a little investigating. But as long as David and Maddie worked together, yet didn't *get* together, America didn't care if they ever got to the bottom of a case. So what if there were occasional launches into lunatic fancy—like the Elizabethan "Taming of the Shrew" episode, the '40s-style film noir pastiche, the frequent into-the-camera asides. It was all fine and dandy, as long as the mile-a-minute dialogue kept coming, and the potent emotions that coursed between the Blue Moon detectives stayed under the surface where they belonged. Unfortunately, David and Maddie *did* get together, late in *Moonlighting*'s run, and the show lost its fizz. ✦ But while it was good, it was great. And hey, that Al Jarreau theme song rocked. —MARC BERNARDIN

SHINE OF THE TIMES: THE FEISTY P.I. PAIR UPDATED NICK AND NORA FOR THE STYLISH '80S

THE AVENGERS

THIS SPY TEAM BOWLERED US OVER

BEFORE MULDER AND SCULLY, before David and Maddie, before Sam and Diane, they were the King and Queen of Unresolved Sexual Tension: John Steed and Emma Peel of the semi-serious '60s British spy drama *The Avengers.* The two were like James Bond squared—a debonair male agent who shared an ongoing flirtation (but not a bed, as far as we could make out) with a sexy female associate very much his equal. Maniacal masterminds, psycho scientists, even a giant man-eating plant—all were swiftly dispatched with a minimum of fuss. Never has saving the world been carried off with such exquisite savoir faire. ✦ On the surface, Patrick Macnee (Steed) and Diana Rigg (Peel) were something of an odd couple. Consider their wardrobe choices: The aristocratic Steed verged on dandyism with his omnipresent three-piece Savile Row suit, bowler, and umbrella, while Peel favored the Carnaby Street look, reporting to work in zippered, skintight leather pantsuits and high-heeled boots, perfect for the high-kicking karate moves she was often called on to execute. Yet pheromones definitely flew whenever Steed laid one of his quips on "Mrs. Peel" (a widow, you see) and she smiled back coquettishly, tossing a loosely curled lock of black hair off a perfect cheekbone. Faced with Rigg's charms, even the iciest of British reserves dissolved into puddles. ✦ In 1968, just two years after *The Avengers* started airing in the U.S. on ABC, someone rained on this cool couple's parade: Mr. Peel. (It turns out the long-lost test-pilot hubby still drew breath.) Rigg left the show, replaced by the bustier, more obvious (and only half as much fun) Linda Thorson. But in the hearts of untold legions of male admirers on both sides of the Atlantic, Mrs. Peel—the Femme Nikita of her age—lives on. —NANCY BILYEAU

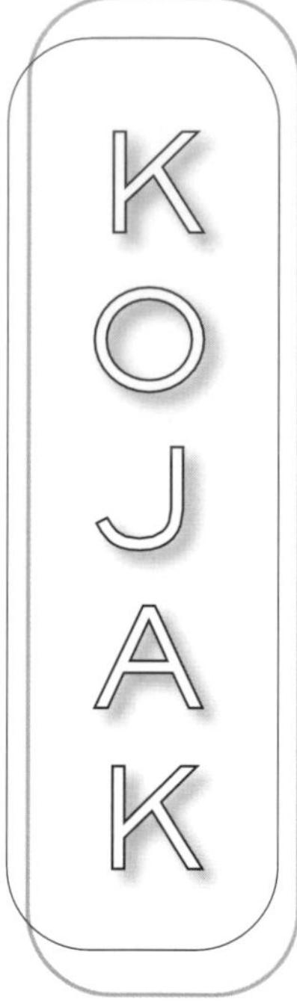

KOJAK

THE MAKERS OF ROGAINE have good reason to hate Telly Savalas. As tough-guy New York City police lieutenant Theo Kojak on CBS' *Kojak* from 1973 to 1978, the actor actually succeeded in making male baldness sexy. (He also did great things for lollipop sales and the image of tough Greek-American cops.) But Savalas' most enduring achievement may have been injecting a much-needed shot of heart into the formulaic police dramas of the mid-'70s. With its grim tales of desperate New Yorkers enmeshed in tangled criminal webs, *Kojak* put a human face on the cops-and-robbers genre, placing the emphasis on gritty, realistic characterization and setting the stage for such shows as *Hill Street Blues*. ✦ *Kojak*, which was adapted from the 1973 made-for-TV movie *The Marcus-Nelson Murders*, was an instant hit with fans, who responded to Savalas' steely-eyed magnetism and cynical persona as much as to the compelling story lines. Savalas, who had played villains for most of his career, brought a faintly malevolent spark to his cop role. "I'll scatter your brains from here to White Plains," he threatened a thug in one episode. Yet for all his barely suppressed rage, Kojak solved crimes with his head more often than with his gun, giving the lie to those critics who carped that the show was just one more example of gratuitous violence on the tube. ✦ Savalas had a trademark existential question he asked in nearly every episode: "Who loves ya, baby?" The answer, where *Kojak* was concerned, is obvious: anyone who cared about great dramatic television. —TOM SINCLAIR

SAVALAS' MACHO COP BALDLY WENT WHERE '70S POLICE SHOWS HAD NEVER GONE BEFORE

CAGNEY & LACEY

TWO TOUGH-AS-NAILS WOMEN MADE THE STREETS SAFE FOR EQUAL-OPPORTUNITY CRIME FIGHTING

BUSTED! HARD AS IT IS to believe, this '80s cop drama actually had two things in common with '70s jiggle-fest *Charlie's Angels*: Barney Rosenzweig (*C&L*'s exec producer had cut his teeth on *Angels*), and the women-as-detectives format. Of course, that's where all similarities end. Recovering alcoholic Chris Cagney (Sharon Gless) and mother of three Mary Beth Lacey (Tyne Daly) would never have been caught dead in hot pants and chains—this crime drama took its two female leads *very* seriously. ✦ But not at first: Rosenzweig had conceived *C&L* as a big-screen comedy about two female buddy cops; after every major studio (and then all three networks) rejected that idea, he sold CBS on a dramatic TV movie (with *M*A*S*H*'s Loretta Swit as Cagney). It did so well that CBS ordered six episodes of the new series, only to quickly pull the plug (for one thing, some saw lesbian overtones between Daly and Meg Foster, Swit's replacement). By fall 1982, the more conventionally feminine Gless had replaced Foster, but flat ratings prompted CBS to cancel the series again. That's when the fans stepped in, launching a letter campaign that (along with four Emmy nods) persuaded CBS to give *C&L* one more chance in March 1984; this time, it landed in the top 10. ✦ What was all the fuss about? Viewers tuned in not just to see two women cops bring the bad guys to justice, though that in itself was still a novelty. They watched because *C&L* offered one of the most complete pictures to date of two women and the issues they faced: abortion, child abuse, sexism, rape. As cocreator Barbara Corday has said: "Cagney and Lacey are two women who happen to be cops. They are not two cops who happen to be women. Being cops was never what it was all about." Whatever *C&L* was about, it sure made for some arresting TV. —SHAWNA MALCOM

JUST THE FACTS

KOJAK

YEARS ON AIR 1973–78

TOP NIELSEN CHARTING 7th (1973–74)

EMMYS WON 1 (Savalas for Best Actor in a drama)

BALD AMBITION Savalas came to acting relatively late—age 35—after working for the State Department.

STEP UP TO THE PATE Savalas first shaved his head to play Pontius Pilate in 1965's *The Greatest Story Ever Told.*

HORSE SENSE Savalas invested some of his *Kojak* earnings in a racehorse, which he named Telly's Pop.

TELLY TUNES The star recorded an album in 1975 called *Telly*, which included his cover of "You've Lost That Lovin' Feeling."

A FRIEND IN NEED Savalas was the godfather of *Friends*' Jennifer Aniston.

BALD MOVE *Homicide*'s Andre Braugher played Kojak's sidekick in ABC's 1989–90 revival of the cop series.

CAGNEY & LACEY

YEARS ON AIR 1982–88

TOP NIELSEN CHARTING 10th (1983–84)

EMMYS WON 14

NAME-DROPPERS While developing the script in the 1970s, cocreators Corday and Barbara Avedon called the project *Newman & Redford,* after the male buddy stars of *Butch Cassidy and The Sundance Kid* and *The Sting.*

AN EYE FOR THE TALENT Rosenzweig's marriage to Corday ended in divorce; he went on to marry Gless.

THE RIGHT CHOICE The National Right to Life Committee requested that CBS preempt an episode in which Lacey reveals that she'd had an abortion as an unwed teenager, or else air the committee's 30-minute anti-abortion film *Matter of Choice.* The network refused.

JUST THE FACTS

MIAMI VICE

YEARS ON AIR 1984–89

TOP NIELSEN CHARTING 9th (1985–86)

EMMYS WON 4

ORIGINAL CASTING Anyone but Don Johnson. He had starred in a succession of failed TV pilots, and NBC feared *Miami Vice* might fizzle if he were cast in a leading role.

PRESCIENT CASTING A guest spot as a weapons-trading baddy was one of Bruce Willis' few TV roles before being cast in *Moonlighting*. In the original pilot, Jimmy Smits was cast as Crockett's partner.

ART IMITATES LIFE For realism, *Miami Vice* scripts occasionally borrowed from actual Miami narcotics investigations, and its cast sometimes included real-life Florida drug kingpins.

VISUAL CUES Producer Michael Mann dictated that there be no earth tones in the show; he would also bring a water truck to shooting locations to wet down the streets so that they would glisten on camera.

MAGNUM, P.I.

YEARS ON AIR 1980–88

TOP NIELSEN CHARTING 3rd (1982–83)

EMMYS WON 2

THE INSPIRATION CBS had built large production facilities in Hawaii during the years *Hawaii Five-0* was on the air and wanted to find some way to make use of the investment.

THE MAN BEHIND THE CURTAIN The owner of the estate, Robin Masters, was never seen on camera. From 1981 to 1985, his voice was supplied by Orson Welles.

CAMEOS The producers landed Frank Sinatra (as a retired New York police sergeant) for a rare guest appearance.

WONDERFUL ACTING Hillerman's performance as the veddy British Higgins was a pose: The actor was born in Texas.

WHAT DID THEY KNOW? "The producers will be very lucky if one wag or another doesn't promptly dub the series *Magnum P.U.*" –*The Washington Post*, Dec. 11, 1980

FERRARIS? LINEN AND LOAFERS? SURE—THEY WERE THE COOLEST COPS UNDER THE SUN

MIAMI VICE

FROM UNDER HIS LOOSE linen jacket peeks a lime green T-shirt. His pants are unbelted. No socks. Hasn't shaved in two days. On the way to work he slips a Glenn Frey cassette into his Ferrari tape-deck player and "You Belong to the City" blares from the speakers as he zooms down the palm-tree-lined causeway. Gee, it was a tough life, being a homicide detective in Miami, circa 1985. ✦ The ultimate elevation of style over substance, *Miami Vice* was born when NBC programming czar Brandon Tartikoff uttered the fateful words "MTV cops" to producer Michael Mann, who took the idea very, very seriously. The music (Lionel Richie, the Rolling Stones), the wardrobes (pastels only), the hipster guest stars (from Bianca Jagger to G. Gordon Liddy), the rain-slicked noirish streets—Mann lavished time and money (upwards of $1 million per episode) on each and every detail. ✦ And then there were the stars: Don Johnson, as living-on-the-edge cop Sonny Crockett, and Philip Michael Thomas, as his equally pouty partner, Ricardo Tubbs. Two little-known actors who found it hard to keep their heads when the show exploded in the ratings: Johnson became a tabloid sex symbol, with the world held hostage to his courtship of and remarriage to Melanie Griffith; Thomas compared himself to Gandhi, telling an interviewer, "I don't mind walking with the people." ✦ All the hype and hoopla came to an end when Mann, like a child hungering for new toys, jumped to the big screen, later directing *The Last of the Mohicans*. After sinking to 53rd place in 1989, *Vice* slunk into the south Florida sunset. ✦ Luckily, for those still yearning for some mid-'80s magic, the show lives on. At its Florida theme park, Universal Studios has a *Miami Vice* attraction, complete with speedboats, helicopters, and Crockett and Tubbs look-alikes fleeing huge explosions. How's that for livin' on the edge? —NB/PHOTOGRAPH BY GARY NULL

MAGNUM, P.I.

THIS ISLAND INVESTIGATOR DOLED OUT JUST AS MUCH SEX APPEAL AS SLEUTHERY

PETER FALK. TELLY SAVALAS. Robert Blake. All whizzes in the sleuthing department but, let's face it, hardly *GQ* cover boys. In fact, not until Tom Selleck, ex-*Dating Game* contestant and Salem cigarette man, stepped into the scuffed sneakers of Vietnam War vet Thomas Magnum did the detective-show genre land its first bona fide hunk. The strapping (6-foot-4), dimpled Selleck exuded a good-guy sex appeal that drew women to what had been almost exclusively male territory. ✦ And unlike Jack Lord's granite-jawed character on *Magnum, P.I.*'s predecessor, *Hawaii Five-O*, Selleck brought to his crime-solving efforts a laid-back sartorial style (a Detroit Tigers cap, loud Hawaiian shirts unbuttoned down to *there*), an endearing fallibility (he'd outrun the bad guys only to forget where he'd parked the getaway car), and, most notably, a healthy sense of tongue-in-cheek humor (what other show would bring in comedienne Carol Burnett to share a bank vault with Magnum in a case gone awry?). ✦ After all, we didn't tune in to this *Rockford*-esque drama for its weekly dose of suspense. It was Selleck's amiable charm, and the incessant bickering with his tightly wound British majordomo, Jonathan Higgins (or "Higgie Baby," as Magnum called him), that kept Americans watching. As played by John Hillerman, Higgins appeared perpetually annoyed, but we knew he secretly delighted in the errant private eye's company. And who could blame him? Magnum packed one helluva Hawaiian punch. —SM

HYPER-COMPETENT? RIGOROUSLY FAIR? TV'S ORIGINAL DEFENSE ATTORNEY IS GUILTY AS CHARGED.

PERRY MASON

PERRY MASON HAS A LOT TO ANSWER FOR. After dozens of novels, several movies, a 12-year radio serial, and finally the classic 1957-66 CBS series starring Raymond Burr, Erle Stanley Gardner's implacable defense attorney came to seem the very idea of what the public wanted of lawyers. We esteem him still: A 1993 survey ranked the fictional Mason second on a list of lawyers Americans admire most—after F. Lee Bailey but before any of the Supreme Court justices. ✦ No wonder the legal profession is so roundly despised—how can anyone hope to compete with a guy who won 270 out of 271 televised cases? (For the record, Mason's one "loss" came in 1963's "Case of the Deadly Verdict"—but he later exonerated his client after finding the real criminal.) Quite probably, we responded to Mason because, in show after show, he acted more like a detective than an attorney—chasing down witnesses, sending investigator Paul Drake (William Hopper) out to dig the dirt, bringing his physical and moral bulk to bear in the climax so that the real murderer just had to stand up in court and shriek, "All right! So I killed him!" ✦ Or maybe we just caught Mason at the right moments: When actor Burr was cornered by a fan who demanded to know why he won every case, he responded, "But Madam, you only see the cases I try on Saturday." It's worth noting, too, that we only saw the cases in which he defended attractive white people. Reality was never on trial in *Perry Mason*; on the contrary, with the real world spinning increasingly out of control, the show assured viewers that crime could be contained, in an hour, in black and white, and always with the right verdict. —TY BURR

PERRY MASON

YEARS ON AIR 1957–66

TOP NIELSEN CHARTING 5th (1961–62)

EMMYS WON 3

CODE OF ETHICS Creator Gardner allegedly required that all of Mason's clients be innocent, and that all be acquitted. He also prohibited Mason from engaging in "innuendo of flirtation" and from being violent.

ORIGINAL CASTING The producers' first choice for Mason was Fred MacMurray (he didn't want to work the long hours); Rod Serling was also reportedly considered.

PRESCIENT CASTING Both Robert Redford and Dustin Hoffman appeared as witnesses in separate episodes.

HOW HE GOT THE PART Portly Burr was up for the role of the district attorney but allegedly went on a crash diet to make himself more credible as the dashing Mason.

CAMEOS In the final episode of the original *Perry Mason* television series, Gardner played the judge. When Burr was recovering from surgery in 1963 and was temporarily unable to appear on the series, Bette Davis was one of three "guest attorneys" who filled in for him.

LEGALESE Burr had to deliver so many lines in each episode that *Perry Mason* supposedly became one of the first shows to use a TelePrompTer on the set.

SPIN-OFFS *The New Perry Mason*, a 1973 CBS show with a new cast that lasted only 15 episodes; *The Return of Perry Mason*, a series of new television movies with most of the original cast, which began appearing on NBC in 1985

PEYTON PLACE

THAT OTHER PLACE, the one Heather Locklear prowls in stiletto heels, wasn't even a glimmer in Aaron Spelling's eye when its prototype debuted in 1964. *Peyton Place*, based on Grace Metalious' 1956 best-seller about the goings-on in a small New England town, took a bag of sins (backstabbing, murder, blackmail), mixed in a little sex (okay, a *lot* of sex), and, before you could say catfight, the prime-time soap was reinvented. ✦ From the start, critics were appalled ("We'll review it as soon as the nausea passes," remarked one). Talk-show hosts were licking their chops (Johnny Carson declared it "the first TV series delivered in a plain wrapper"). And viewers? They were loving every minute of it. In fact, so feverishly did fans embrace *Place* that before long, the half-hour melodrama was snagging 60 million viewers an episode, paving the way for sudsers from *Dallas* to *Dawson's Creek*. ✦ It wasn't Chekhov, but it *was* irresistible. Thirty years before a pregnant Amanda came between Billy and Allison on *Melrose*, a pregnant Betty (Barbara Parkins) came between *Peyton*'s star-crossed couple, rich kid Rodney Harrington (Ryan O'Neal) and good girl Allison MacKenzie (Mia Farrow). Betty miscarried, natch, but didn't tell Rodney for fear he'd desert her for Allison. By the time Farrow left to wed Frank Sinatra after the second season, the show's popularity was already on the wane. Neither Rodney nor *Peyton* ever quite recovered. No matter: For a brief, golden time, *Peyton Place* was a deliciously wicked stay. —SM

THIS TAWDRY TALE SPAWNED A DYNASTY OF PRIME-TIME SOAPS

ALFRED HITCHCOCK PRESENTS

A MASTER OF THE MACABRE, HE GAVE US THE BIG CHILL

JAMES CAMERON HOSTING a network anthology of seafaring tales? Martin Scorsese emceeing tonight's Mafia miniseries? Unthinkable. Yet from 1955 to 1965, while directing some of the greatest psychological thrillers of all time—*Vertigo, North by Northwest, Psycho*, and *The Birds*—the "master of suspense" hosted TV's *Alfred Hitchcock Presents*, an anthology of weekly half-hour and then one-hour episodes. ✦ Admittedly, Hitchcock personally directed only 20 of the series' 362 mini-dramas. But the spirit of Hitch was everywhere. He selected the material, often adaptations of short stories by preeminent writers like H.G. Wells, John Cheever, and Ray Bradbury. He picked the directors, giving a shot to newcomers Robert Altman, Sydney Pollack, and William Friedkin. And he cast many of the shows with future A-list actors like Robert Duvall, Robert Redford, Gena Rowlands, and Burt Reynolds. ✦ When it came to plot structure, the man who shocked audiences by killing off Janet Leigh just a third of the way through *Psycho* insisted on plenty of twists and turns. A classic episode featured a rejected wife (Barbara Bel Geddes) who whacks her hubby with a frozen leg of lamb, then serves the cop searching for the murder weapon a home-cooked meal: lamb, of course. ✦ It was his CBS show that imprinted the Hitchcock persona on much of the public: his portly profile, his taste for black comedy and sight gags (he liked to introduce episodes with, say, a noose around his neck), and his sepulchral "Good e-e-e-evening." Best of all, he bit the hands that fed him, insulting advertisers by drawling "Of course, just as no rose is complete without thorns, no show is complete without the following..." Sponsors were outraged. But they calmed down after discovering the jokes actually gave their products a perverse cachet. As always, that final twist. —NB

JUST THE FACTS

PEYTON PLACE

YEARS ON AIR 1964–69

TOP NIELSEN CHARTING 9th (1964–65)

EMMYS WON 1

MILKING IT *Peyton Place* was the first prime-time series to appear more than one night a week. Within a year, hit-starved ABC had upped the pace to three nights a week.

KEEPING BANKERS' HOURS Dorothy Malone agreed to play Constance MacKenzie for $7,000 a week (rather than the $10,000 ABC offered) in exchange for a guarantee that she would be off the set by six each night and have weekends off.

REVERSE PSYCHOLOGY Perhaps the best publicity was the banning in 1956 of the novel on which it was based in Providence, Omaha, Fort Wayne, Ind., and Canada. In spite (or perhaps because) of this brouhaha, the book's sales outstripped even *Gone With the Wind*'s.

HAPPY ENDINGS When the show was canceled, frustrated Dutch TV viewers had some of the cast flown to Holland, where they shot a finale.

ALFRED HITCHCOCK PRESENTS

YEARS ON AIR 1955–65

TOP NIELSEN CHARTING 6th (1956–57)

EMMYS WON 3

MUSIC FOR THE MACABRE The theme song, Gounod's "Funeral March of a Marionette," was selected personally by Hitch, who said, "I'm the marionette, you see, that's the whole point of it."

NOT KEEPING THE CENSORS HAPPY The network refused to air one episode from the original series (about a mentally retarded boy who watches a magician saw someone in half, and decides he'd like to do the same).

EXPORTING MAYHEM With an eye toward international distribution, Hitchcock's introduction to each show was filmed in German and French, as well as English.

REPLACEMENT PARTS Most of the crew for Hitchcock's classic film *Psycho* came from the television series.

WITH THIS FALLIBLE DETECTIVE HEROINE, YOU GET THE TRUTH, THE WHOLE TRUTH, AND NOTHING BUT THE TRUTH

PRIME SUSPECT

IN A TV UNIVERSE FILLED with perky lifeguards, wisecracking nannies, and nail-gnawing career girls, Helen Mirren's Detective Chief Inspector Jane Tennison, of PBS' *Prime Suspect*, cuts through all the nonsense like a saber. The fiercely ambitious Tennison is whip-smart—but she's also irritable and manipulative. The hemlines of her aggressively plain suits fall a good foot below Ally McBeal's; her lank, indifferently cut blond hair frames a face lined by too many late nights of toil, not to mention a fondness for drink and cigs. As a police supervisor surrounded by hostile males, she'd be well advised to steer clear of workplace romances, but she has bedded both a subordinate and a boss—and regretted both. In short, she seems like a living, breathing human—a TV commodity all too rare. ✦ Watching Tennison do her thing—tracking down and then wringing a confession from a murder suspect—is like watching a tightrope artist performing without a net. There's simply no way to anticipate how the Emmy-winning Mirren will play a scene (which has more than a little to do with the fearless actress' talent for shock—she's appeared in such classics of kink as *Caligula* and *The Cook, the Thief, His Wife & Her Lover*). It also doesn't hurt that many episodes of the intermittent series are deftly written by crack British-crime novelist Lynda La Plante or that the suspects themselves are often played by exceptional thespians like David Thewlis and Ciaran Hinds. ✦ Tennison doesn't always get it right in the end; occasionally, the suspect eludes arrest. But that, as any *Prime Suspect* aficionado could tell you, is quite beside the point. —NANCY BILYEAU

LAW & ORDER

'LAW & ORDER' IS TESTIMONY to the power of a great concept. How else could a series survive after its entire original cast had left? With its ingeniously simple structure—in the first half hour, police book 'em; in the second half hour, prosecutors cook 'em—new characters could be easily added. Thus, as the veteran NYPD detective, George Dzundza was replaced by Paul Sorvino, who was replaced by Jerry Orbach; and Benjamin Bratt stepped in for Chris Noth in the junior-cop role. But from the 1990 pilot, one character remained constant (no, not Steven Hill's terminally dyspeptic DA, Adam Schiff—he didn't appear until the series' second episode): New York City. Shot on location, *L&O* has always captured the Big Apple's unmistakably bitter flavor, its story lines often ripped from the local tabloids ("Murders in Central Park!" "Preppie Rapists!"). Initially, NBC's *L&O* seemed downright monkish with its all-male cast and ascetic aversion to delving into its characters' private lives (a characteristic perhaps best personified by Michael Moriarty as all-work-and-no-play ADA Ben Stone). But things loosened up as women joined the cast in 1993 and the showier Sam Waterston took over for Moriarty in 1994; slowly, we began to learn more about the characters (for example, Carey Lowell's ADA, Jamie Ross, fought for custody of her kid). Despite the cast changes, as the years passed, *L&O* became more successful—and respected. In its seventh season, the show was a top 30 staple and copped its first Emmy for best drama. It was a long-overdue reward for one of TV's most captivating, underrated pleasures. —BF/PHOTOGRAPH BY PAUL DRINKWATER

NEW YORK CITY IS THE REAL STAR OF THESE TORN-FROM-THE-TABS CRIME STORIES

JUST THE FACTS

PRIME SUSPECT

YEARS ON AIR 1992–98

TOP NIELSEN CHARTING Not available

EMMYS WON 1

HOW IT ALL BEGAN Writer Lynda La Plante, who first suggested the idea of a realistic crime drama with a female homicide investigator to Brit TV execs, found that the London police had only four women at the supervisory rank of detective chief inspector.

CASTING NOTES Mirren was the only actress considered as Tennison but reportedly was told to cut the beautiful blond hair for which she was known.

TIPS FROM THE PROS Mirren researched the role of Tennison by talking to London police officers. Two things she learned were "Never let them see you cry" (for obvious reasons) and "Never fold your arms" (because it's defensive body language).

LAW & ORDER

YEARS ON AIR 1990–present

TOP NIELSEN CHARTING 25th (1995–96)

EMMYS WON 5

WHERE THEY GOT THE IDEA In the '60s, ABC aired a similar series, *Arrest and Trial*, in which the first half was devoted to catching the bad guys and the second half to getting a conviction.

A MAN OF HIS WORD Moriarty loudly criticized Attorney General Janet Reno for decrying TV violence, then quit in protest and announced he was running for President (two days later, he withdrew his candidacy).

RELIGIOUS CONVICTIONS Steven Hill, a practicing Orthodox Jew, refuses to work during the Sabbath, Friday sundown to Saturday sundown.

LOCATION, LOCATION, LOCATION The *L&O* studio sits on a Hudson River pier that was once home to *Kojak* and *The Equalizer*.

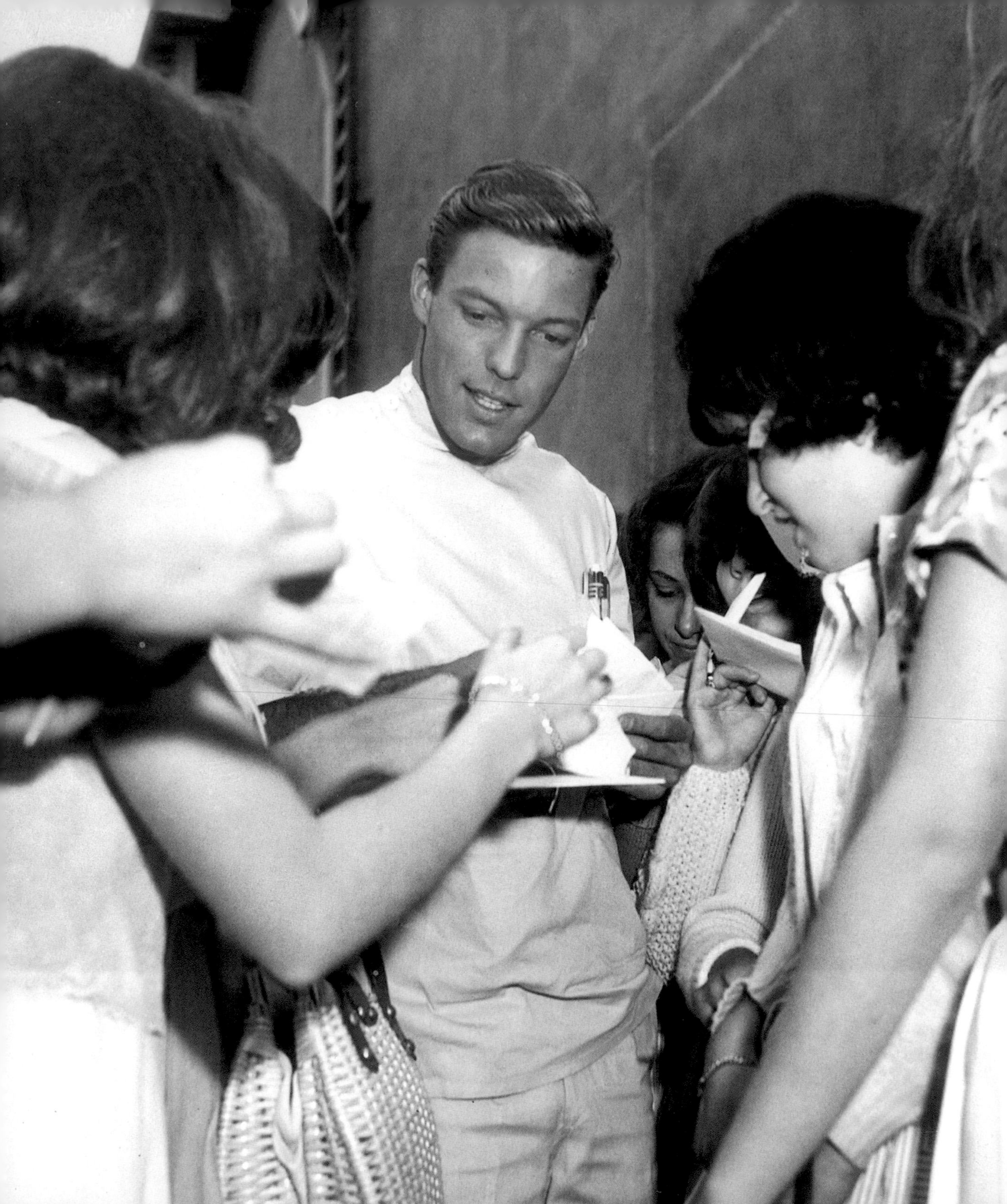

JUST THE FACTS

DR. KILDARE

YEARS ON AIR 1961–66

TOP NIELSEN CHARTING 9th (1961–62)

EMMYS WON 0

WHERE THEY GOT THE IDEA A series of Max Brand's (*Destry Rides Again*) short stories were made into *Kildare* films (most with Lew Ayres as Kildare and Lionel Barrymore as Dr. Gillespie).

HYPOCRITIC OATH Publicists reportedly claimed that Chamberlain was as squeaky-clean as Kildare—that he never smoked, drank, or cussed. Once he left the show, the actor admitted to enjoying all of the above.

ORIGINAL CASTING William Shatner turned down the offer to play Kildare.

THE SINGING PHYSICIAN Chamberlain's vocal version of the *Dr. Kildare* theme song became a top 10 hit in 1962.

WHAT'S UP, DOC? Viewers reportedly wrote Chamberlain asking for medical advice.

COLUMBO

YEARS ON AIR 1971–78

TOP NIELSEN CHARTING 14th (1971–72, 1973–74; as part of the *NBC Mystery Movie* series)

EMMYS WON 9

WHERE THEY GOT THE IDEA The character of Columbo was based in part on Petrovich, the detective in *Crime and Punishment*.

ORIGINAL CASTING The title role was first offered to Lee J. Cobb, who turned it down, after which Bing Crosby was considered (he preferred the golf cours then was the part of Lie Columbo offered to Falk

INCUBATING TALENT Some episodes were w Steven Bochco (*Hill Str* *L.A. Law*) and Stephen (*The Rockford Files, Wi*

THE GAME OF THE NA In seven years, the lieu first name was never re

CAST OF CHARACTER himself was the only re character—all others va after just one episode.

DR. KILDARE

TV'S HANDSOME YOUNG DOC HAD FEMALE FANS LINING UP FOR AN APPOINTMENT

LONG BEFORE GEORGE CLOONEY wielded his prime-time stethoscope on *ER*, the dashing Dr. James Kildare (Richard Chamberlain) was giving legions of female viewers heart palpitations with his portrayal of a young intern beginning his career at a large city hospital. By milking the potential for high-stakes human drama and life-and-death story lines endemic to medical series, *Dr. Kildare* (whose title character had been through several incarnations in print, on radio, and on film) would become one of prime time's first successful doctor shows. ✦ Each week, under the watchful eye of his beetle-browed mentor, Dr. Leonard Gillespie (Raymond Massey), Kildare grappled with the dilemmas of his patients, always going that extra mile for problem cases (and often even injecting himself into troubled family lives). He would have been the tube's undisputed top doc were it not for ABC's rival series, *Ben Casey*, which starred Vince Edwards as a tough, rather simian-looking sawbones who stood in stark contrast to Chamberlain's squeaky-clean heartthrob character (if *Dr. Kildare* was the Beatles of medical shows, *Ben Casey* was the Rolling Stones). ✦ Alas, in its final season (when the show switched from black and white to color), *Dr. Kildare* underwent several changes that sealed its fate: Formerly an hour-long affair, the program was split into two half-hour episodes that aired on consecutive nights, and given a more soap opera-ish, serial quality. A predictable love interest for Kildare, head nurse Zoe Lawton (Lee Kurty), was also introduced. But apparently no amount of surgery, cosmetic or otherwise, could save this terminally ill show, and in August 1966, NBC pulled the plug. —TOM SINCLAIR

COLUMBO

BENEATH THAT SHLUBBY COAT AND BUMBLING MANNER LAY ONE OF TV COPDOM'S SHARPEST MINDS

NO GUNS. NO SEX. NO COSTARS. A lot more talk than action. A mystery whose solution appears...at the beginning? A decidedly unheroic-looking detective who doesn't even show up in the first segment? It's a wonder NBC's suits ever even allowed this crime drama on the air. But *Columbo*'s creators, Richard Levinson and William Link, knew what they were doing: Those apparent anomalies went a long way toward making their show a TV classic. ✦ The key to *Columbo*'s enduring allure, of course, was the good detective himself, first written as a minor character in Levinson and Link's play *Prescription: Murder* and brought quirkily to life by Peter Falk. Arriving on the scene of a homicide in his hoary Peugeot jalopy, clad in a rumpled raincoat and chomping on a cigar, Falk's bedraggled Lieutenant Columbo (what was his first name anyway?) was a seasoned LAPD vet whose *dems*-and-*dese* patois hinted at a New York birthright. He also appeared a tad, well, scatterbrained. ✦ But therein lay the real treat of every *Columbo* episode. By the time his cocksure adversaries realized that behind Columbo's slouchy mien lay a steel-trap deductive mind, it was too late. The plots were more like turtle-and-hare races than cat-and-mouse games, with the inevitable turning of the tables providing *Columbo*'s delicious payoffs. ✦ Though without a supporting cast, Falk was aided and abetted by a stellar stable of guest villains, including Robert Culp, Ruth Gordon, William Shatner, Johnny Cash, and Falk buddy John Cassavetes (who played a mistress-murdering conductor). A second pal, Ben Gazzara, was one of the show's crack directorial alumni, who also included Jonathan Demme and, for the very first *NBC Mystery Movie* series installment, a struggling would-be auteur named Steven Spielberg. ✦ Oh, yeah, one more thing. *Columbo* snagged 9 Emmys over its original seven-year run, three of which were best actor nods for Falk. Nothing mysterious about that. —MIKE FLAHERTY

FAMILY

WHO SAID THE BURBS HAD TO BE BORING?

BEHIND THE BLANDEST OF TITLES lies one of TV's richest and most powerful prime-time hours. *Family* took one seemingly harmonious California family and examined the struggle and pain beneath its suburban surface. ✦ Sound like the usual Sturm und Drang found on many a nighttime soap? Sure. *Family* routinely ventured into movie-of-the-week land with plotlines revolving around drug use, abortion, adoption, and illness. But the show managed to rise above soapsville: touching, not touchy-feely, loving but never lame. ✦ Maybe the key to its perfect pitch was in the credits. With Aaron Spelling and Mike Nichols among its executive producers, one can imagine a sort of dramatic checks and balances at work—the former's penchant for potboiler wrestling with the latter's considered realism. (Later, two alums, Ed Zwick and Marshall Herskovitz, created another critical hit, *thirtysomething*.) ✦ It didn't hurt, of course, that the producers had an ace ensemble, most notably the wonderful Sada Thompson. As Kate Lawrence, she mixed strength and sensitivity to create a whole new kind of TV matriarch. Rounding out the cast were James (father of Matthew) Broderick, Meredith Baxter Birney, Gary Frank, and, of course, Kristy McNichol, as the adorable Buddy. ✦ *Family* brought touchy material to the screen with rare force and maturity. Its humanity—and a nervy willingness to forgo happy endings—was its hallmark. —MF

THIRTY-SOMETHIN

TO THE WHINIEST BUNCH IN TV HISTORY: ANGST FOR THE MEMORIES

JUST AS FEW PEOPLE LABEL themselves yuppies without a self-conscious shrug, few viewers proudly defined themselves as fans of *thirtysomething* during the show's 1987-1991 run. So much self-analysis, so much anxiety over marriage and kids, so much ambivalence over careers, so much...well, whining. ✦ The mission statement of creators Ed Zwick and Marshall Herskovitz was itself pretty wince-worthy: "This is a show about life on earth as we know it. At least a small slice of it. It's about a group of people, all of a certain age, who know enough about life to be totally confused by it. It's about growing up—no matter how old you are." As the petulant young Ethan Weston would wail: "Yuck!" ✦ Yet if you worked through the cringe factor, *thirtysomething* yielded real rewards. The ongoing saga of two married couples (Nancy and Elliot Weston, and Michael and Hope Steadman) and three singles (Ellyn Warren, Melissa Steadman, and Gary Shepherd) living in Philadelphia, the show boasted top-drawer writing and acting. ✦ More than a few of its plotlines hit real nerves. When Nancy (Patricia Wettig), long-suffering, insecure wife of the flaky infidel Elliot (Timothy Busfield), underwent treatment for ovarian cancer, viewers were transfixed—and Wettig won two well-deserved lead-actress Emmys. Of subtler stuff was the gradual decline of the Steadman marriage, from nauseating coziness to sexual boredom to bitter estrangement (in the series' finale, the couple, played by Ken Olin and Mel Harris, very nearly separated). ✦ But in a show revolving around intimate relationships, it was a plot arc set in the workplace that, oddly enough, proved the most riveting. After Elliot and Michael's boutique advertising business failed, they went to work for rival Miles Drentell (David Clennon), a Machiavellian ad guru who clearly relished tormenting the two boy-men. For anyone who has nervously toiled under a manipulative boss, this was can't-miss TV. Which gets to the point of *thirtysomething*'s impact: Few other shows, either before or since, have even attempted to chronicle the daily lives of middle-class boomers. And that, despite all the eye-rolling about self-obsessed yuppies, is a real shame. —NB/PHOTOGRAPH BY JIM SHEA

JUST THE FACTS

FAMILY

YEARS ON AIR 1976–80

TOP NIELSEN CHARTING Never cracked the top 25

EMMYS WON 4

PRIME-TIME POLITICS By the late 1970s, each of the three nets wanted an hour-long family drama on the schedule. CBS had *The Waltons*; NBC had *Little House on the Prairie*; ABC came up with *Family*.

UNWHOLESOME RIVALRY Gary Frank, who played *Family*'s idealistic teen Willie, said of *The Waltons*: It's about "11 people who have all had frontal lobotomies."

WHERE THEY GOT THAT SNAPPY TITLE After the pilot had been completed, Nichols joked that the show should be called *Acceptable for the Family Hour*. The show aired well outside the family hour, at 10 p.m., where it beat the very popular *Kojak*.

LET'S CALL THEM THE QUIETS Aaron Spelling and Leonard Goldberg said the idea for *Family* came to them when they recalled PBS' 1973 documentary about a Santa Barbara family called the Louds.

THIRTYSOMETHING

YEARS ON AIR 1987–91

TOP NIELSEN CHARTING Never cracked the top 40

EMMYS WON 11

ABOUT THE TITLE *thirtysomething* was written as one word to imply togetherness; it was written in lowercase letters to invoke e.e. cummings and his hip disregard for authority.

GROUNDBREAKING MOMENT *thirtysomething* was the first network series to show a gay couple in bed together. This bit of daring cost ABC $1.5 million in advertising for the episode.

TOUCHY-FEELY MILESTONE Psychologists have shown *thirtysomething* episodes to their patients as part of their therapy.

POP-CULTURE OBSESSIONS One episode has Michael grappling with religious doubt by entering a Dick Van Dyke fantasy world; Zwick and Herskovitz named their production company Bedford Falls after the town in *It's a Wonderful Life*.

DRAGNET

THANK GOD IT'S FRIDAY (HARD-BOILED COP JOE FRIDAY, THAT IS)

PRODUCER, WRITER, and—in his own uniquely wooden fashion—actor Jack Webb was Sgt. Joe Friday, a Los Angeles cop with a funereal mien and a clipped manner of speaking. "Just the facts, ma'am" became his trademark phrase, but years of comedians parodying Sgt. Friday have left *Dragnet* underrated as one of the finest police shows ever. Its best episodes were police procedurals as stark as any film noir (it's a good bet that feature director Robert Aldrich learned a thing or two from Webb in making his classic 1955 hard-boiled movie, *Kiss Me Deadly*). ✦ The series was distinguished by its relentless realism—crime solving not as a glamorous cat-and-mouse game but as a more tedious process of endless interviews, file research, and small lucky breaks. Fact-based ("The story you are about to see is true. Only the names have been changed to protect the innocent" was a voice-over mantra attached to

every episode) and slowly paced, *Dragnet* was everything television isn't in the '90s; its very slowness gives it an almost avant-garde allure today—it's like *Twin Peaks* without the weirdness. ✦ In many people's memories, Webb's partner was the equally deadpan Bill Gannon, played by Harry Morgan (who would go on to greater fame as Col. Sherman Potter on *M*A*S*H*), but Gannon didn't show up until the show's second run, beginning in 1967. It's the series' '50s episodes, however, that hold up as classics of blunt police drama. —KT

BEFORE 'I SPY,' the prospect of a black actor costarring in a network-TV series was as unlikely as, say, a sitcom featuring an out-of-the-closet lesbian. But with the Sept. 15, 1965, premiere of this adventure-espionage drama, at least one aspect of Dr. Martin Luther King Jr.'s dream came to fruition as the small screen got its first African-American costar, a neophyte actor named Bill Cosby. The show teamed Cosby, then known primarily as a stand-up comic, with veteran actor Robert Culp as the globe-hopping salt-and-pepper duo of Kelly Robinson (Culp) and Alexander Scott (Cosby), American undercover agents with a knack for defusing dangerous situations with light, improvised banter. (The Scott role was not specifically written for a black actor, but executive producer Sheldon Leonard opted to go with Cosby after catching the comedian's routine on a Jack Paar special.) Aside from being a civil rights landmark, *I Spy* was novel in that it was one of the few series—then or now—to be shot in exotic locations rather than on a Hollywood back lot. Each week, the agents traveled to Spain, Greece, Hong Kong, and elsewhere, giving *I Spy* a unique and refreshing international flavor that provided a deft counterpoint to Robinson and Scott's easy, cross-racial camaraderie. The partners' chummy on-screen rapport spilled over into real life, and they reunited for an *I Spy* TV movie in 1994. (Cosby, who won three Emmys for his work on the original show, has said he always felt bad that Culp was never similarly honored.) ✦ Though it went off the air three decades ago, *I Spy*'s importance as a vehicle for social change cannot be underestimated. With its implicit message of brotherhood and interracial cooperation, this popular, fast-paced little spy show probably did more to advance race relations than a hundred protest marches, proving that, at its best, television can educate as it entertains.

—TOM SINCLAIR/PHOTOGRAPH BY ALLAN GRANT

I SPY

COSBY AND CULP'S ESPIONAGE ESCAPADES MADE FOR THE FIRST TRUE BLACK-AND-WHITE SERIES

JUST THE FACTS

DRAGNET

YEARS ON AIR 1952–59; 1967–70

TOP NIELSEN CHARTING 2nd (1953–54)

EMMYS WON 5

WHERE THEY GOT THE IDEA *Dragnet* started as a radio show that almost didn't make it to TV because NBC executives felt it "didn't resemble Sam Spade enough."

ARMED BUT NOT DANGEROUS Webb would allow only one bullet to be fired every four episodes.

NOT ONLY ARE THE STORIES TRUE...but people involved in the actual crimes often played walk-on roles in the episodes that dramatized them.

FRIDAY TAKES A FALL At the conclusion of the first television version of *Dragnet*, Friday was promoted to lieutenant. When the subsequent *Dragnet 67* premiered, he had been mysteriously demoted back to sergeant.

FALLEN HERO When Webb died in 1982, the LAPD flew its flags at half-staff.

I SPY

YEARS ON AIR 1965–68

TOP NIELSEN CHARTING 29th (1966–67)

EMMYS WON 3

IT WASN'T ALWAYS SUCH A WONDERFUL LIFE *I Spy* was produced by former actor Sheldon Leonard, who played the bartender who throws George Bailey (Jimmy Stewart) out of his roadhouse in *It's a Wonderful Life*.

NOT SWEATING THE CHURCH-AND-STATE STUFF While the show was on location, much of its footage was shot by NBC news crews.

EQUAL-RIGHTS BILL NBC fretted about how Southern affiliates would react to Cosby having equal billing with Culp. The network was particularly concerned about both men sitting in the front seat of a car together, or staying in the same hotel.

IVY LEAGUE CACHET Culp's character was supposed to be a former law student at Princeton. The problem is, Princeton has no law school.

GUTS AND GLORY: CRICHTON'S FAST-PACED MEDICAL SAGA DELIVERS THE GOODS

'ER' TOOK THE MEDICAL DRAMA and gave it a shot of adrenaline. Not for nothing did one of its resident directors, Mimi Leder, become an action filmmaker (*The Peacemaker*, *Deep Impact*). With stretchers crashing through doorways, blood spurting from wounds, and life-and-death crises unfolding, the NBC show packs all the excitement of a summer-movie blockbuster. But unlike so many event pictures, *ER* has heart underneath its heroics. The soul of the series is Dr. Mark Greene (Anthony Edwards), who helps run the

JUST THE FACTS

ER

YEARS ON AIR 1994–present

TOP NIELSEN CHARTING 1st (1995–96, 1996–97)

EMMYS WON 12

THE NAME IS FAMILIAR One of Clooney's previous credits is *E/R*, a sitcom that starred Elliott Gould. It lasted one season (1985–86) and was also set in the emergency room of a Chicago hospital.

ORIGINAL TITLE *EW* (for Emergency Ward) was the title of Crichton's 1974 screenplay on which the series is based.

TOUCH OF REALITY The production staff culls medical stories for *ER* from real-life incidents at emergency rooms across the country.

TANGLED HISTORY Steven Spielberg originally wanted to produce Crichton's script as a movie but then became more interested in producing (and directing) Crichton's *Jurassic Park*. An exec of Spielberg's company Amblin Television came across the script and pitched it as a TV series.

PRODUCTION NOTES Each episode of *ER* takes eight days to shoot (20 days from preproduction to air date); as a result, several episodes are in production at any one time throughout the season.

emergency room at an inner-city Chicago hospital. Though beset by numerous travails (his wife left him, he was beaten by a thug), Greene retains an inner decency that pervades the show. As Greene's best pal, smooth-operating pediatrician Doug Ross, George Clooney has ridden *ER* to big-screen stardom, but the rest of the cast is no less charismatic. Julianna Margulies has skillfully evoked nurse Carol Hathaway's slow emotional recovery after a suicide attempt; Eriq LaSalle has resisted the temptation to turn prickly surgeon Peter Benton into a cuddly curmudgeon; Noah Wyle has subtly transformed John Carter from a naive med student into a confident doctor; Gloria Reuben has refused to allow HIV-positive physician's assistant Jeanie Boulet to be portrayed as a pitiful victim. *ER* was an instant smash, proving the Midas touch of co-creator Michael Crichton (who based the series on his own memories of medical school). Yet viewers stayed with the show because of its compassion and intelligence—the two most important qualities of a good doctor.

—BF/PHOTOGRAPH BY LARA JO REGAN

JUST THE FACTS

TWIN PEAKS

YEARS ON AIR 1990–91

TOP NIELSEN CHARTING 21st (1989–90)

EMMYS WON 2

SELF-PORTRAIT FBI agent Cooper is reportedly based on creator Lynch.

PRESCIENT CASTING David Duchovny as transvestite Fed Denise/Dennis Bryson

THINKING THE UNTHINKABLE The pacing of the first *Twin Peaks* was so unlike any other TV show that had come before it, ABC briefly considered airing a full hour without commercial interruptions.

WELL, LA-DEE-DA Diane Keaton directed one episode.

LOCATION, LOCATION, LOCATION Much of the show was filmed in Snoqualmie Falls, Wash., which has since become a mecca for fans.

THEY DIDN'T LIKE *DALLAS*, BUT... *Twin Peaks* was all the rage when shown in Japan.

MISSION: IMPOSSIBLE

YEARS ON AIR 1966–73

TOP NIELSEN CHARTING 11th (1968–69)

EMMYS WON 6

WHERE THEY GOT THE IDEA Inspired by 1964's *Topkapi*, producer Bruce Geller originally conceived of *Mission* as a movie.

THE PRICE IS RIGHT Each episode cost $225,000 to produce and used up 50,000 feet of film (twice the average for an hour-long series).

THIRD-WORLD BAD GUYS TAKE NOTE By its third season, *Mission* was being aired in 69 countries and 15 languages. This is thought to have created an exaggerated impression of the CIA's abilities.

TEMPUS FUGIT One of the show's trademarks was the "quick insert"–a brief image of dripping water or a ticking clock used to increase tension. Some episodes contain up to 100 of these shots.

REPLACEMENT PARTS Martin Landau–who had turned down the role of Spock in *Star Trek*–was replaced by Leonard Nimoy when Landau left *Mission* in 1969.

THIS RIDDLE WRAPPED IN A MYSTERY WAS AS SATISFYING AS, WELL, A GOOD CUPPA JOE

TWIN PEAKS

WHEN THE CORPSE known as Laura Palmer—naked, wrapped in plastic, bluish, and beautiful—first turned up in the Pacific Northwest town of *Twin Peaks* on April 8, 1990, she breathed new life into the genre of TV drama. ✦ *Peaks* sprang from the twisted psyches of David Lynch, the man behind such disturbing cinematic nightmares as *Eraserhead* and *Blue Velvet*, and Mark Frost. The series focused on the death of Palmer (Sheryl Lee), a deceptively innocent prom queen, and the ensuing FBI investigation by Agent Dale Cooper (Kyle MacLachlan), who unearthed the sinister evils hidden in the seemingly tranquil town. ✦ Like all of Lynch's work, *Peaks* wasn't afraid to make audiences switch on their brains and open themselves up to a little discomfort. The stylized images (an executed mynah bird's blood splattered on rows of perfectly stacked doughnuts, a hysterical father being lowered into the grave on top of his daughter's coffin) and off-putting plot devices (Cooper often got his leads from a backward-speaking dwarf who appeared to him in dreams) were sometimes nonsensical—and always creepy. Still, the fiercely loyal cult following that quickly sprang up around *Peaks* proved that America was aching for a sexy and surreal crime-genre alternative to the doddering detectives (i.e., Benjamin Matlock and Jessica Fletcher) of the day. ✦ While the hype surrounding the series premiere was immense, the numbers and network support soon dwindled, and *Peaks* crumbled in April 1991 (a two-hour finale would air in June). Even so, Agent Dale Cooper can take comfort in knowing that his journeys into the depths of spookyville were reborn three seasons later with a new pair of FBI renegades—Mulder and Scully. —KRISTEN BALDWIN/

PHOTOGRAPH BY CRAIG SJODIN

MISSION: IMPOSSIBLE

THE SECRET-AGENT DRAMA, IF YOU CHOSE TO ACCEPT IT, WAS ONE WILD, JINGOISTIC RIDE

THIRTY YEARS on, it may be hard to recall individual story lines of *Mission: Impossible* with any real clarity, but the CBS show's distinctive opening remains etched in the consciousness of anyone who ever saw it. Each week, the leader of the Impossible Missions Force, James Phelps (Peter Graves)—or, for the first season, Daniel Briggs (Steven Hill)—listened to a tape recording on which an officious-sounding voice gave him details about a proposed, very dangerous assignment—so dangerous that the spiel always ended with the less-than-comforting words "Should you or any member of your IM Force be caught or killed, the secretary will disavow any knowledge of your actions. This tape will self-destruct in five seconds." Then the tape would go up in smoke, and the hyperactive theme music would kick in. Face it: No matter what followed, that dramatic dispensation to each mission was nearly impossible to top. ✦ Plots were fairly complex (though nowhere near as impenetrable as the 1996 Tom Cruise film), usually involving the Force's infiltration of some obscure foreign country. Sticky spy work, like setting up dictators for a fall or stealing documents, was performed by a team that included electronics expert Barney Collier (Greg Morris), strong-arm man Willie Armitage (Peter Lupus), and, for three seasons, sexpert Cinnamon Carter (Barbara Bain) and master-of-disguise Rollin Hand (Bain's husband, Martin Landau). Characters were pretty much stick figures—but who cared? The show ran on the adrenaline generated by the high-wire tension the team constantly worked under. ✦ Some said the series was morally objectionable, a bit of jingoistic propaganda that painted all foreigners as villains. But in truth, the IMF probably wasn't doing anything that hadn't already occurred to the CIA or FBI. (Say, do you suppose the government kept a file on this show?) —TS

JUST THE FACTS

LITTLE HOUSE ON THE PRAIRIE

YEARS ON AIR 1974–83

TOP NIELSEN CHARTING 7th (1977–78)

EMMYS WON 3

SMALL WORLD The spot where the real Ingalls family home stood in the 1860s is part of a Kansas farm on which newsman Bill Kurtis (of A&E fame) grew up.

OFFBEAT CASTING Former Los Angeles Rams star Merlin Olsen as Jonathan Garvey

SPIN-OFFS After Landon left the NBC series (but stayed on as producer), it continued for one season under the title *Little House: A New Beginning.* There were three TV-movie reunions: *Little House: Look Back to Yesterday* (which evoked a strange degree of nostalgia for a series that had left the air just a few months earlier); the deceptively titled *Little House: The Last Farewell*; and the real, honest-to-God last installment, *Little House: Bless All the Dear Children.*

THE WALTONS

YEARS ON AIR 1972–81

TOP NIELSEN CHARTING 2nd (1973–74)

EMMYS WON 11

ORIGINAL CASTING Henry Fonda, the producers' first choice to play John Walton in the TV movie that spawned the series, had played the father in the 1963 movie *Spencer's Mountain,* which was also based on Hamner's recollections.

PRESCIENT CASTING John Ritter (who would leave to star in *Three's Company*) played Reverend Matthew Fordwick the first five seasons.

"NICE" DEPRIVATION The Waltons seemed a tad comfy for a Depression-era rural family. Hamner's original production notes insisted "there should be no hint of squalor or debased living conditions usually associated with poverty."

FAMILY BUSINESS *The Waltons* was the first series from Lorimar, which would later give us the similarly squeaky-clean *Eight Is Enough,* as well as *Dallas.*

HOME SWEET HOMESTEAD: WHO'D HAVE THOUGHT THE FRONTIER WAS SUCH FUN?

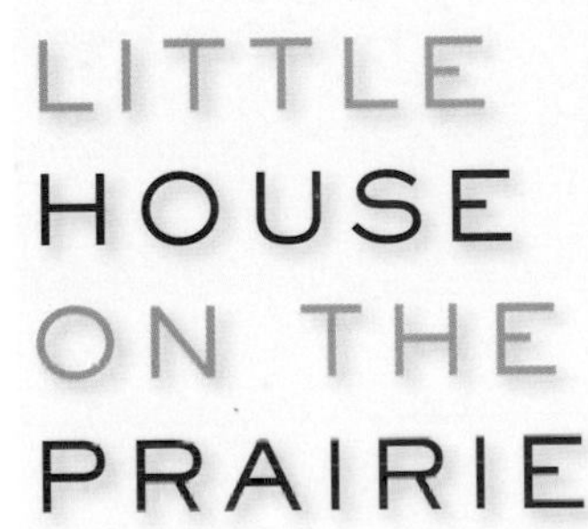

WHEN IT WAS AT LAST TIME for Michael Landon (*Bonanza*'s hotheaded Little Joe) to settle down and become an even-tempered family man, he couldn't have picked a purtier little homestead than *Little House on the Prairie*. Fireside chats, muslin pinafores, burbling creeks, romps over the plains under this patriarch's beatific gaze—such were the idyllic rites of passage for Melissa Gilbert, who, as Laura Ingalls, grew from bucktoothed, pigtailed, lisping cutie to smooth-browed teacher and wife of the strapping Almanzo "Manny" Wilder (Dean Butler). Whatever scrapes she got into, Laura was always essentially the "good" girl, facing off with naughty nemesis Nellie Oleson (Alison Arngrim in blond boing-boing curls). Laura's sister Mary, played by Melissa Sue Anderson, was even more a model of goodness (insufferably so, until she went blind in the fourth season). ✦ The girls' sun-dappled Walnut Grove, Minn., circle would wax and wane, but you could always count on a one-room schoolhouse, a kindly reverend, and a dose of morality by hour's end. If the series wasn't always faithful to the real Ingalls Wilder's beloved children's books (who *was* that Albert character, anyway?), it still was burnished with enough 1870s log-cabin ambiance to masquerade as a bona fide history lesson. And considering that the series aired during the divorce-torn *1970*s, it's not surprising that the ruggedly old-fashioned Ingalls family home felt like such a peaceful refuge. For eight years under Landon's thoughtful stewardship, this was a *House* you pined to return to. Until an 11-year-old Shannen Doherty appeared on the scene as Almanzo's saucy niece, that is. Those really *were* the days. —ALEXANDRA JACOBS

THE WALTONS

THE YEAR: 1972. CBS' MISSION: coming up with a new Thursday-night series to beat the pants off of ABC's too-cool-to-live *The Mod Squad* and NBC's wildly wacky *Flip Wilson Show*. Its solution: *The Waltons*, a no-frills drama about a proud family eking out a living on a Virginia mountain during the depths of the Depression. Few laughs. No miniskirts. Not a star in sight. ✦ *Huh?* was the collective response. This was a time when family fare meant the laugh-tracked escapades of sunny suburban clans like the Partridges and the Bradys. Yet CBS stuck by the series when its early ratings languished in the Nielsen basement, running newspaper ads asking America to "Save the Waltons." ✦ And, by golly, America did. The show caught on, eventually beating its competition before peaking at No. 2. More than a decade before family values became a rallying cry, *The Waltons*, based on the life story of novelist Earl Hamner Jr., delivered just that: At the end of every show, before dropping off to sleep, the seven kids (including series star John-Boy, played by Richard Thomas), their parents (Ralph Waite and Michael Learned), and their grandparents (Will Geer and Ellen Corby) made a touching family chorus out of the simple phrase "Good night." ✦ *The Waltons* became such a favorite that years after its 1981 cancellation, its name still evoked a certain "Let's gather in front of the fire" spirit: In 1992, President Bush said he wanted to "make American families a lot more like the Waltons and a lot less like the Simpsons." Could John-Boy ever trump Bart in viewers' hearts? For a sweet, uncynical stretch in TV history, maybe, just maybe. —MMF

DEPRESSION ASIDE, THIS FAMILY WAS RICH WITH LOVE

NYPD BLUE

THE TITLE ISN'T JUST an allusion to cocreators Steven Bochco and David Milch's previous cop-show masterpiece, *Hill Street Blues*. It's a cheeky pun to boot: *NYPD* is the bluest show in prime-time history. But the controversial cusswords and bare butts were merely a come-on to get curious viewers to tune in to a truly mature drama, one that features fully fleshed-out characters grappling with such tough issues as racial prejudice, prostate cancer, domestic violence, and alcoholism. ✦ When *NYPD* premiered on ABC in 1993, it made instant sex symbols out of a pair of unlikely mugs: redheaded, pale-faced David Caruso (as perpetually simmering Det. John Kelly) and bald, potbellied Dennis Franz (as his deeply irascible partner, Andy Sipowicz). The headlines about *Blue*'s "adult content" were soon replaced, however, by stories about Caruso's temperamental on-set behavior; his departure early in the second season raised questions about the show's future. But Jimmy Smits (who had worked with Bochco on *L.A. Law*) seamlessly segued into the lead role of Det. Bobby Simone, a widower whose grief was assuaged by his romance with fellow cop Diane Russell (Kim Delaney). ✦ With *NYPD*, Bochco built on the groundbreaking *Hill Street*, bringing the cop show into the '90s with evocative dialogue and first-rank acting. Yet *Blue*'s episodes are also throwbacks to an earlier era of sprawling urban tableaux like *The French Connection* and *Prince of the City*—with TV now offering the kinds of great, gritty crime dramas that movie studios don't make anymore. —BF/PHOTOGRAPH BY MICHAEL GINSBURG

BOCHCO'S LATEST SMASH IS STILL A MAGNUM FORCE

HOMICIDE: LIFE ON THE STRE

WITH KILLER PLOTS AND DEAD-ON PORTRAYALS OF THE GOOD, THE BAD, AND THE UGLY, THIS IS A CRITICAL FAVE TO DIE FOR

"WE STARTED OUT to do a show that deals with the aftereffects of murder, rather than watching a murder and chasing the action," explains *Homicide: Life on the Street* executive producer Barry Levinson. "We turned the camera in the opposite direction and said the real drama is in the humanity and the loss of life." Set in Levinson's hometown of Baltimore and featuring a squad of cops as chatty as the characters in his films *Diner* and *Tin Men*, *Homicide* also established a shaky-cam style that initially made viewers seasick but soon trickled into the mainstream. ✦ Of course, *Homicide* has never been a breakout hit, perhaps because it so strenuously avoids falling into familiar TV formulas. One week, the story is seen from the point of view of the criminals instead of the cops. Another episode features flashbacks to the '30s, as the detectives reopen Baltimore's oldest unsolved mystery. Plotlines can be intensely condensed (a man pushed in front of a subway train dies as Andre Braugher's Det. Frank Pembleton searches for his killer) or epically long (the murder of young Adena Watson has haunted Kyle Secor's Det. Tim Bayliss since the 1993 pilot). ✦ Although the show suffered a shockingly high turnover rate (nine regulars exited in the first six seasons), the quality of its scripts—overseen by *St. Elsewhere* vet and executive producer Tom Fontana—has remained remarkably high. "There's a concerted effort to reinvent the show," says Fontana. "None of us ever wants to feel like we've made the perfect *Homicide*." Maybe not, but they've come pretty damn close. —BF/PHOTOGRAPH BY LARRY FINK

JUST THE FACTS

NYPD BLUE

YEARS ON AIR 1993–present

TOP NIELSEN CHARTING 8th (1994–95)

EMMYS WON 14

ORIGINAL CASTING Smits, who joined the cast in its second season, was Bochco's first choice for Detective Kelly.

ART IMITATES LIFE Many story lines in the first seasons were provided by real NYPD Det. Bill Clark, who was a creative consultant on the show, later moving to coexecutive producer after he retired from the police force. Detective Simone uses Clark's old badge number: 3118.

SIPOWICZ IN THE JUNGLE Franz turned to showbiz after surviving combat in Vietnam.

FROM OLD BLUE TO 'NYPD BLUE' TV is cocreator David Milch's other career. He has also taught English literature at Yale.

WHAT DID THEY KNOW? "Bochco hits bottom with *NYPD Blue*.... This is Bochco's emptiest series yet." –*The Boston Globe*, Sept. 10, 1993

HOMICIDE: LIFE ON THE STREET

YEARS ON AIR 1993–present

TOP NIELSEN CHARTING 27th (1993–94)

EMMYS WON 2

WHERE THEY GOT THE IDEA The NBC series is based on David Simon's book *Homicide: A Year on the Killing Streets*, a day-by-day chronicle of 12 months in a Baltimore homicide squad.

LIFE SURRENDERS TO ART In 1996, a fleeing shoplifter ran into the middle of a *Homicide* rehearsal. Thinking he was surrounded by real police, he gave up.

CINEMA ENERVATÉ *Homicide* achieves its unique visual style by filming each scene from start to finish with one camera, then filming it again with the camera at a slightly different angle. The two shots are then intercut, and overlapped slightly. This technique is called stutter-step.

OOPS! Searching for a place that looked like a crack house, production executives once stumbled upon a real crack house.

JUST THE FACTS

MAVERICK

YEARS ON AIR 1957–62

TOP NIELSEN CHARTING 6th (1958–59)

EMMYS WON 1

WHERE THE NAME COMES FROM The word *maverick* means "an individual who does not go along with a group or party"; it derives from 1860s Texas rancher Samuel A. Maverick, who refused to follow the near-universal practice of branding cattle, thinking it cruel.

MAKING A VIRTUE OF NECESSITY Early episodes featured Garner as the only male lead. Because each show was taking eight days to produce, Warner Bros. introduced Jack Kelly as Garner's brother, Bart. Doing more than one episode simultaneously (alternately focusing on Garner and Kelly) helped the production stay on a weekly schedule.

THE DECLINE OF THE WESTERN WORLD By *Maverick*'s second season, 7 of the top 10 shows on TV were Westerns.

THE RIFLEMAN

YEARS ON AIR 1958–63

TOP NIELSEN CHARTING 4th (1958–59)

EMMYS WON 0

HOW IT ALL BEGAN Writer-director Sam Peckinpah (who would later become famous for such ultraviolent Western movies as *The Wild Bunch*) wrote a *Gunsmoke* script about a rifle-toting frontiersman and his son that was rejected. He sold a revised version as the pilot for *The Rifleman*.

PREVIOUS CAREER HIGHLIGHTS Crawford was a onetime Disney Mouseketeer; Connors had played professional basketball for the Boston Celtics and major-league baseball for the Brooklyn Dodgers and the Chicago Cubs.

SUBSEQUENT CAREER HIGHLIGHTS Crawford would later become a real cowboy of sorts, performing in a professional rodeo.

MAVERICK

FLUSH WITH IRREVERENT WIT, THESE WILD-WEST JOKERS SHOT FROM THE LIP—AND GARNERED RAVES

A SLY PARODY OF CONVENTIONAL Westerns, *Maverick* fully lived up to the implications of its name, juicing genre clichés with wry humor and offbeat plots, in the process inventing a whole 'nother kind of cowboy show. James Garner was the wisecracking cardsharp Bret Maverick, as unlikely a Wild West hero as one could hope for. A professed coward who shied away from physical confrontation, Maverick, who was something of a con man, preferred brainpower to gunpowder (he wasn't much good with firearms, anyway). One of the "pappyisms"—bits of wisdom handed down to him by his father—Maverick was fond of spouting was "Love your fellow man, and stay out of his troubles if you can," a bromide that summed up his worldview nicely. ✦ Garner's all-too-human character and understated comedic touch struck a bull's-eye with viewers, who loved *Maverick* for its subversive novelty. Especially sidesplitting were the ABC series' occasional spoofs of other TV shows (*Gunsmoke*, *Bonanza*, and *Dragnet* were all given the *Maverick* treatment, with hilarious results). Following a contract dispute with Warner Bros. Studios, Garner hightailed it off the show after three years (1957-60), never to return. Jack Kelly, who played series regular Bart Maverick (Bret's brother), stepped in, alternating with Roger Moore (Cousin Beauregard Maverick) as the principal character. In the spring of '61, a third Maverick sibling, Brent (Robert Colbert), was introduced, but by then much of the magic was gone. By July 1962, so was this odd little gem of a show. —TOM SINCLAIR/PHOTOGRAPH BY JON BRENNEIS

PERVERSELY GRIM AND disarmingly gentle, *The Rifleman* was an anomaly among the herd of TV Westerns in the late '50s and early '60s. A forerunner of Clint Eastwood's *Unforgiven*, it followed a lanky stranger named Lucas McCain (Chuck Connors) as he tried to settle down in post-Civil War New Mexico. Lucas had a gun, of course—a Winchester .44-40 action rifle with a hair trigger and a "special hoop lever." Damned if we know what that is, but it meant that he could fire off eight rounds in 2.5 seconds, which brought every punk in the West around to test his luck. ✦ What Lucas also had—and what gave ABC's *The Rifleman* its unusual gravity—was a young son, played by Johnny Crawford (who briefly and somewhat improbably became a real-life singing idol as time went on). Somber to a fault, the series showed Lucas trying hard to be both father and mother to the boy, and that air of throttled emotionalism—invariably dispelled at the climax by the blam-blam-blam of Lucas' rifle—made for one strange Western. ✦ It was an intentionally odd mix from the start. Producer Arnold Laven had found himself at a dead end with the pilot's script, in which loner Lucas loses a shooting match to save his own skin. Then one day, as Laven kissed his young son goodbye, the answer came to him: If Lucas had a child, he'd look like a good father instead of a lousy hero. The key, the producer recalled later, was "a kind of moral point of view that came out of my own feelings about raising my son. The show was within the top five within the second or third week." —TY BURR

THE RIFLEMAN

IN ITS FATHER-SON FOCUS, THIS SOMBER WESTERN HIT THE MARK

L.A. LAW

GORILLA SUITS? VENUS BUTTERFLIES? WELCOME TO THE '80S, PERRY MASON.

IN THE MID-'80S, greed was good on Wall Street—and in the glittering canyons of L.A., where Steven Bochco set his upscale tale of a high-gloss law firm. Slick and polished, NBC's *L.A. Law* was the epitome of Reagan-era entertainment, as the chronically self-involved attorneys at McKenzie, Brackman set out to make money (tightfisted managing partner Douglas Brackman), get laid (perpetually randy divorce specialist Arnie Becker), or wrestle their consciences into submission (sensitive litigator Michael Kuzak). With this crew of conniving counselors, Bochco at last ripped the fig leaf off traditional TV portrayals of the legal profession. ✦ And we loved it. The show was a success in its inaugural year, finishing in Nielsen's top 25 during its first five seasons. Bochco's *Hill Street Blues*-honed storytelling style got us hooked on the firm's power struggles, the lawyers' chaotic home lives, and cases both outlandish (dwarf tossing) and in synch with current issues (insurance coverage for AIDS patients). What's more, Bochco and partner Terry Louise Fisher spiced up the mix with a dash of good old-fashioned romance: Kuzak (Harry Hamlin) donning a gorilla suit to claim Grace Van Owen (Susan Dey); Stuart Markowitz (Michael Tucker) winning the heart of Ann Kelsey (Jill Eikenberry) through the Venus Butterfly. ✦ After the fifth season, ratings fell off as melodrama threatened to lapse into farce (Brackman dating Vanna White—please!); it was like watching an eminent barrister turn into an ambulance chaser. Thankfully, in the final season, the creators returned to the things that had once made the show great, reminding us that at its best, *L.A. Law* was topical but not preachy, sexy but not soapy—a skillful blend of the attorneys' trials and their tribulations. —CAREN WEINER

"I'M STILL AMAZED when people talk about *St. Elsewhere*," says producer Tom Fontana. "At the time, we were just trying to do it. We never sat back and went, 'God, we're really contributing to television history.'" But they were. Without *St. Elsewhere*, there would be no *ER*. Earlier hospital dramas like *Ben Casey* and *Marcus Welby, M.D.*, had portrayed doctors as medical supermen who rarely, if ever, lost their patience—or their patients. What *Hill Street Blues* (also produced by MTM) had done for TV cops, NBC's *St. Elsewhere* did for TV docs: It humanized them. ✦ Boston's St. Eligius—sarcastically nicknamed St. Elsewhere because of its reputation for taking cases no other hospital wanted—housed a fascinat-ingly flawed staff: Dr. Mark Craig (William Daniels) was a heartless heart surgeon with a failing marriage; Dr. Peter White (Terence Knox) was a rapist who was killed by a nurse; Dr. Robert Caldwell (Mark Harmon) was a womanizer who once had to have his member surgically removed from his zipper and later contracted AIDS. ✦ *St. Elsewhere*'s ever-changing ensemble cast ranged from the sublime (Denzel Washington and Alfre Woodard as young doctors in love) to the ridiculous (prop comic Howie Mandel and *Animal House* alum Stephen "Flounder" Furst as hapless sophomoric M.D.'s). Its story lines similarly merged deadly serious issues (cancer, suicide) with darkly comic subplots, several of them involving Florence Halop as perennial patient Mrs. Hufnagle, who died in a freak hospital-bed accident. ✦ The writing staff of *St. Elsewhere*—who would later work on such top-quality dramas as *Homicide: Life on the Street, Chicago Hope, Northern Exposure*, and *NYPD Blue*—turned out dazzlingly inventive scripts. Nowhere was this more apparent than in the surreal finale, when it was suggested that the whole show had been a hallucination by Tommy Westphall (Chad Allen), the autistic son of the hospital's ex-chief of staff, Dr. Donald Westphall (Ed Flanders). Thankfully, though, *St. Elsewhere* was no hallucination for TV viewers. —BF/PHOTOGRAPH BY BUD GRAY

THIS DOC DRAMA BREATHED NEW LIFE INTO THE MEDICAL GENRE

ST. ELSEWHER

JUST THE FACTS

L.A. LAW

YEARS ON AIR 1986–94

TOP NIELSEN CHARTING 12th (1987–88)

EMMYS WON 18

ROMAN A CLEF Series cocreator Terry Louise Fisher is a real-life lawyer who was once a deputy district attorney.

ART IMITATES LIFE Attorney Stuart Markowitz married attorney Ann Kelsey in January 1988. In real life, Tucker and actress Eikenberry (who played Markowitz and Kelsey) had already been married for 15 years.

SPIN-ONS Supervising producer William L. Finkelstein left *L.A. Law* to create the legal drama *Civil Wars* for ABC. When that series was canceled and Finkelstein returned to *L.A. Law*, he imported two characters from the ABC show (Denise Iannello, played by Debi Mazar, and Eli Levinson, played by Alan Rosenberg) into *L.A. Law*.

SLIGHTLY EMBARRASSING PREVIOUS CAREER HIGHLIGHTS Harry Hamlin starred in *Clash of the Titans*; Alan Rachins, in the nude Broadway musical *Oh! Calcutta*.

ST. ELSEWHERE

YEARS ON AIR 1982–88

TOP NIELSEN CHARTING Never broke into the top 40

EMMYS WON 12

GROUNDBREAKING MOMENT Harmon's Bobby Caldwell was the first major character in a prime-time network series to contract AIDS.

POP-CULT OBSESSIONS The public address system at St. Eligius hospital often paged doctors with names like Casey, Zorba, Welby, and Kildare.

ART IMITATES LIFE Bonnie Bartlett (who played the wife of Dr. Mark Craig) was married in real life to William Daniels (who played Craig).

SHORT BUT SWEET The last episode of *St. Elsewhere* was entitled, aptly, "The Last One."

AFTERLIFE The year after *St. Elsewhere* folded, one of the producers went on to create *Tattinger's*, an enormously forgettable hour-long show about the owners of a New York City restaurant.

JUST THE FACTS

WISEGUY

YEARS ON AIR 1987–90

TOP NIELSEN CHARTING Never cracked the top 40

EMMYS WON 0

NOT-SO-MEAN STREETS Although set in New York City (with interludes in Miami and Los Angeles), *Wiseguy* was filmed in Vancouver because production costs there were a fraction of those in Manhattan.

WE KNEW HIM WHEN Wahl describes his "worst job ever" as working cleanup in a Chicago public hospital. He quit and headed for Los Angeles, eight months later landing his first role, the lead in the 1979 cult-film hit *The Wanderers*.

WHAT DID THEY KNOW? "Coming from [producer Stephen J.] Cannell, *Wiseguy*...is, of course, all sweat and swagger, bullets and babes, breeziness and bravado. Men's bowling teams are advised to schedule their nights around this one." –*Chicago Tribune*, Sept. 16, 1987

THE ROCKFORD FILES

YEARS ON AIR 1974–80

TOP NIELSEN CHARTING 12th (1974–75)

EMMYS WON 5

HOW IT ALL BEGAN A writers' strike threw mid-1970s cop series *Toma* behind schedule. The producers wanted to introduce private eye Jim Rockford for an episode so they could shoot two shows in one week. ABC hated the idea, and Rockford never appeared on *Toma*.

ORIGINAL CONCEPT Initially Rockford was supposed to take only closed cases–a convention that was relaxed as the series progressed.

ORIGINAL CASTING Cannell envisioned Robert Blake in the title role.

HIGH-TECH GIMMICK The opening credits began with the sound of the outgoing message of Rockford's answering machine, his alternative to a full-time secretary.

ART DOESN'T IMITATE LIFE For all of Rockford's good-natured cowardice, James Garner served in the merchant marines and Korea.

WISEGUY

LIKE HIS NAME (TERRANOVA), THIS UNDERCOVER AGENT BROKE NEW GROUND

ON CRIME SHOWS, there had always been the good guys and the bad guys, and nothing in between. Until *Wiseguy*. It's tragic bordering on sacrificial that the CBS show was so short-lived, because it was truly ahead of its time. Sure, it had the usual dose of gritty murder and mayhem, but it also managed to be unusually poignant: Ken Wahl's Vinnie Terranova ventured deep into the lives of society's presumptive scum of the earth, so deep that he often felt a complex empathy, even affection, for them. "It wasn't about cops and robbers," said creator Stephen J. Cannell. "It was all about the seduction of Vinnie Terranova—this guy's moral center and what was happening to his compass." ✦ It helped that the seducing was being done by such powerhouse guest actors. Who can forget Ray Sharkey's ruthless Mob kingpin, Sonny Steelgrave, or Kevin Spacey's depraved arms dealer, Mel Profitt, or Jerry Lewis' embattled garment-industry exec, Eli Sternberg? Or the music-biz plot that starred not only Tim Curry and Paul Winfield, but also Mick Fleetwood, Glenn Frey, and Debbie Harry? That type of casting may be de rigueur today, but in the late '80s, recruiting big names for supporting TV roles was a rarity. Also unheard-of was *Wiseguy*'s reliance on "arcs," multi-episode story lines that hooked us for up to 10 weeks; today they're a TV-drama standard. ✦ And if dark, ongoing plots involving government conspiracies and duplicitous bureaucrats seem all too familiar (paging Agents Mulder and Scully), remember: You saw it here first. —MF

ALREADY WELL LIKED by TV viewers for his wiseacre cardsharp Westerner in *Maverick*, James Garner turned that image inside out with NBC's *The Rockford Files*. An independent private eye (and ex-con), Jim Rockford operated out of a dilapidated Malibu house trailer, was always behind on his bills, and was by no measure a heroic hero—he'd just as soon run away from fights with belligerent suspects ("I bruise easy," he cheerfully admitted). ✦ All this made *The Rockford Files* one of the more humorously realistic shows in the detective-storytelling vein. Rockford had a nagging father, Rocky (Noah Beery Jr.); a grudging ally on the LAPD, Sgt. Dennis Becker (Joe Santos); and a semi-dependable snitch in his former jail mate, Angel (Stuart Margolin). The best *Rockford*s were hard-boiled comedies of manners, upending the conventions of the private-eye genre and frequently culminating in Rockford's solving a case in spite of all the foul-ups he'd made throughout the investigation. ✦ Created by producers Roy Huggins and Stephen J. Cannell, *The Rockford Files* managed to have things both ways: It offered sturdily constructed puzzles for plots but gave Garner a grand showcase for some of the finest low-key leading man comedy ever offered in prime time. —KT

STILL A MAVERICK, GARNER GAVE THE SLEUTH GENRE A WRY TWIST

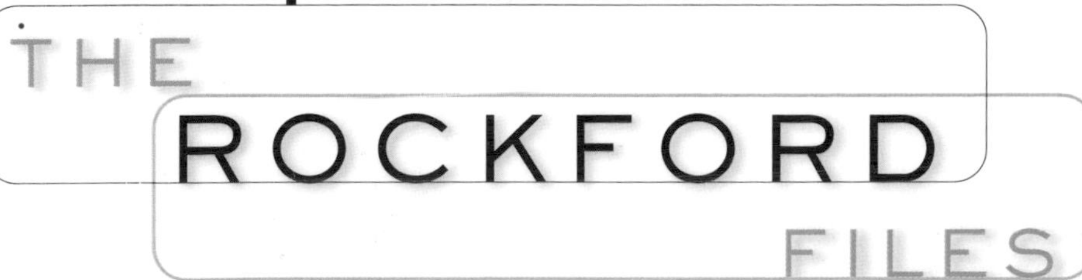

THE ROCKFORD FILES

JUST THE FACTS

RAWHIDE

YEARS ON AIR 1959–66

TOP NIELSEN CHARTING 6th (1960–61)

EMMYS WON 0

ORIGINAL TITLE Exec producer Charles Marquis Warren reportedly considered calling the series *Cattle Drive*.

WHERE THEY GOT THE IDEA *Rawhide* was said to be inspired by the diary of George Dutfield, a cattle driver in the 1860s.

HEY WHO? From 1961 to '64, Robert Cabal played a character whose first name was spelled and pronounced Hey Soos (the English translation is Jesus).

PRESCIENT CASTING Legend has it that Eastwood got the part of Rowdy Yates after being spotted in the CBS commissary by one of the producers.

SLIGHTLY EMBARRASSING PREVIOUS CAREER HIGHLIGHT Sheb Wooley (who played Pete Nolan) had become famous in 1958 for the hit single "The Purple People Eater."

BONANZA

YEARS ON AIR 1959–73

TOP NIELSEN CHARTING 1st (1964–65, 1965–66, 1966–67)

EMMYS WON 2

GETTIN' TOO BIG FOR HIS BRITCHES Pernell Roberts left the series after the 1964–65 season; he loudly denounced it as "junk TV."

THE COLOR OF MONEY *Bonanza* was the first hour-long prime-time series to be broadcast in color. It was rumored that NBC's parent company (RCA)–which was also in the business of selling color televisions–encouraged the change in order to sell more sets.

SLIGHTLY EMBARRASSING PREVIOUS CAREER HIGHLIGHT Michael Landon played the male lead in 1957's *I Was a Teenage Werewolf*.

SPIN-OFFS NBC's 1988 flop *Bonanza: The Next Generation*

BONANZA

GUNS OR NO GUNS, THE PONDEROSA GANG SAT TALL IN THEIR SADDLES

UNKNOWN TO MANY, the classic theme song actually had words: "We've got a right to pick a little fight, Bonanza!" But as a description of the seminal home-on-the-range show, that line couldn't have been more wrong. In the '60s, when riflemen stalked the dusty streets of TV Westerns and gunsmoke filled the air, the men of *Bonanza* used their consciences more often than their six-shooters—and that's what kept viewers coming back to the Ponderosa for 14 years. ✦ Noble father Ben Cartwright (Lorne Greene) had three sons: Adam (original man-in-black Pernell Roberts, who left in 1965), Hoss (gap-toothed giant Dan Blocker), and Little Joe (wiry heartthrob Michael Landon). After hitting a pre-series debut "bonanza" in a silver mine, Ben settled with his sons on a 600,000-acre ranch near Virginia City, Nev. It was the 1860s in the Wild, Wild West—but this was not your average horse opera; with its sensitivity to indigenous rights, contempt for racism (in this case, against Mexicans), and respect for the land, *Bonanza* put a liberal twist on that era. ✦ Which isn't to say the Cartwrights didn't enjoy their share of fisticuffs and gun battles—after all, everyone knew Little Joe was hot-headed as well as hot—but more often than not, their crises were moral ones, like dealing with the theft of a precious war bonnet from an aging Native American chief. Two decades before Kevin Costner won high marks—and Oscars—for racial sensitivity in *Dances With Wolves*, the Cartwright tribe was already trying to do the right thing. —JOE NEUMAIER/ PHOTOGRAPH BY PAUL SELIGMAN

RAWHIDE

WITH CLINT & CO. RIDING HERD, THERE WAS NOTHING STOCK ABOUT THIS DUSTY WESTERN

HAILED AS THE MOST REALISTIC of the many TV Westerns, *Rawhide* answered the question "Where's the beef?" more than two decades before anyone thought to ask it. It wasn't merely that the show focused on the travails of cattle drivers moving herds cross-country; from its CBS debut on Jan. 9, 1959, to its final episode seven years later, *Rawhide* provided an unflinchingly visceral portrait of the hardscrabble lives these men lived. You could almost smell the dust those steers kicked up straight through the TV screen. ✦ The show's stars, too, were tough as year-old jerky: Trail boss Gil Favor (Eric Fleming) could have given John Wayne lessons in all-American machismo, and Wishbone the cook (Paul Brinegar) and Jim Quince (Steve Raines) were no less hard-boiled. (Of course, a damsel in distress could turn any of 'em to mush—and often did during the course of the show's run.) ✦ Although *Rawhide*'s overall excellence is sometimes forgotten, it will certainly be remembered as the show that launched Clint Eastwood's career. Eastwood played the wonderfully named Rowdy Yates, Favor's second-in-command, a ruggedly handsome Young Turk popular with female viewers. After Fleming left the show (and subsequently drowned in a tragic accident), Eastwood even stepped in as trail boss during the show's final days. It seems incredible that a program starring the future Dirty Harry could be canceled unceremoniously in mid-season; the ax nonetheless dropped on *Rawhide* just four months after Eastwood took over the reins. Maybe that explains the Clint squint the actor has put to such potent use ever since. —TOM SINCLAIR

The Thorn Birds

THE BEST MINI-SERIES OF ALL TIME

THE *MINI* IN *MINISERIES* IS ACTUALLY A BIT OF A MISNOMER: SINCE THE GENRE TOOK OFF IN THE MID 1970S, IT HAS PRODUCED SOME OF TV'S GRANDEST AND MOST-WATCHED EPICS. FROM SWEEPING HISTORICAL DRAMAS TO SULTRY FAMILY SERIALS, GOOD MINISERIES ARE A PERFECT EXCUSE TO BECOME AN ANTISOCIAL SHUT-IN BY SPENDING, SAY, 12 HOURS IN FRONT OF THE TUBE. AND TO BE SURE, THERE HAVE BEEN A NUMBER OF GOOD ONES. ON THE FOLLOWING PAGES, KRISTEN BALDWIN PRESENTS *EW*'S CHOICES FOR THE 10 BEST, IN CHRONOLOGICAL ORDER:

The Winds of War

V

The Singing Detective

RICH MAN, POOR MAN *(ABC; debuted Feb. 1, 1976)* One of the earliest network miniseries, *Rich Man* made "novels for television" a viable form of programming. This 12-hour family drama, based on Irwin Shaw's juicy 1970 best-seller, followed the wildly different lives of two brothers: "rich man" Rudy Jordache (Peter Strauss), an ambitious, ultimately corrupt politician wed to his childhood sweetheart (Susan Blakely), and his "poor man" little brother, Tom (Nick Nolte), a part-time boxer and full-time black sheep. Audiences swooned over the relatively unknown Strauss and Nolte, making them superstars and media darlings overnight. Though the Cain-and-Abel saga drew the second-highest share of viewers that season and won three Emmys, a Nolte-less weekly series launched in September 1976 (*Rich Man, Poor Man–Book II*) came up short with viewers.

I, CLAUDIUS *(PBS; debuted Nov. 6, 1977)* What historical era could possibly be more suited to the sweeping miniseries format than the decline and fall of the Roman Empire? The BBC's adaptation of Robert Graves' novels *I, Claudius* and *Claudius, the God* was a darkly comic and randy odyssey into the ancient world's political machinations and sexual indulgences. The 13-part series, airing on *Masterpiece Theatre*, took the form of the memoirs of Rome's fourth emperor, Claudius (Derek Jacobi), an enigmatic figure who used a debilitating stutter to mask a shrewd intelligence. From Augustus and his murderous wife, Livia, to Claudius' troubled reign, which ultimately led to the empire's collapse, *I, Claudius* was lauded for its seamless dramatization of Rome's sordid history—although those bare-breasted orgy scenes *did* raise a few eyebrows.

ROOTS *(ABC; debuted Jan. 23, 1977)* From the minute viewers first met Kunta Kinte—the young, proud, and very frightened African man being taken to America in chains—they were engaged by his story. The bold 12-hour saga, based on author Alex Haley's own family history, followed the lives of Kinte (played by newcomer LeVar Burton), his captors, and his descendants—a star-studded bunch featuring everyone from Cicely Tyson (as Kinte's mother, Binta) to Ed Asner (as a slave-ship captain). While some accused

Roots

Roots of favoring melodrama over historical accuracy, the miniseries was still the first TV program to give the issue of slavery national TV exposure. Like NBC's graphic four-part 1978 miniseries, *Holocaust*, *Roots* got the country talking about an ugly period in human history, and to date no miniseries has equaled its ratings—or its impact.

SHOGUN *(NBC; debuted Sept. 15, 1980)* NBC, together with Paramount, lavished $25 million on this adaptation of James Clavell's 900-page historical novel, and it was money well spent. Richard Chamberlain began his reign as king of the miniseries with his role as the swashbuckling seaman Blackthorne, who is shipwrecked in Japan and befriended by a fierce Japanese warlord (Toshiro Mifune). With its gorgeous panoramic

Rich Man, Poor Man

scenery (all 12 hours were filmed on location in Japan), seductively romantic love story (between Blackthorne and his Japanese interpreter, Mariko), and bloody battle scenes, *Shogun* epitomized the lush historical miniseries. Women across America were left thirsty for more Chamberlain—and they got it, three years later. (See *The Thorn Birds*.)

THE WINDS OF WAR *(ABC; debuted Feb. 6, 1983)* Using World War II as the backdrop for an involved family drama, *Winds* mixed history and Harlequin romance to captivating effect. The 18-hour, $40 million televised version of Herman Wouk's massive 1971 novel followed the war through the eyes of Victor "Pug" Henry (Robert Mitchum), an inconceivably heroic Naval officer who somehow managed to influence all of the war's key players, from Churchill to Roosevelt. What we really tuned in for, though, were the soapy subplots swirling around Pug's family, like the near affair his wife (Polly Bergen) has with a handsome widower, or the romance between his son Byron (Jan-Michael Vincent) and the Jewish beauty Natalie (Ali MacGraw).

THE THORN BIRDS *(ABC; debuted March 27, 1983)* Forbidden love doesn't get any better than this. *Roots* producers David Wolper and Stan Margulies scored again with the four-part story of Father Ralph de Bricassart (Richard Chamberlain) and Aussie enchantress Meggie Carson (Rachel Ward). The two are first drawn to each other when Meggie is a child, having just moved to Father Ralph's parish in the Australian outback. Though the ambitious padre (pushed by Meggie's less-than-saintly grandmother, Barbara Stanwyck) has climbed the ladder of clerical success, he risks it all for his very unpriestly passion for Meggie. Many Catholics denounced the miniseries' Palm Sunday debut as wholly unholy, but nearly 110 million viewers saw at least part of the lovers' saga—Meggie and Father Ralph's consummation in the third installment drew the series' biggest audience—helping to make *Thorn Birds* the second-highest-rated miniseries of its time.

V *(NBC; debuted May 1, 1983)* Science fiction at its moralistic, creepy best, *V* was a chilling allegory on Nazism disguised as a really cool story about lizard-like aliens. Dressed as friendly humans in bright red jumpsuits, the extraterrestrial "visitors" infiltrated earth's major cities with the intention of stealing all our water (and eating all the rodents). Their occupation soon took on fascist overtones, complete with martial law and a youth corps used to expose those who didn't submit. The two-part mini, which shrewdly provided glossy entertainment with a moving Holocaust subtext, ended with the human rebels failing to eradicate the aliens. Viewers returned en masse the next year, when NBC resolved the cliff-hanger (the non-scaly side wins, natch) with *V: The Final Battle*, which will go down in TV history for its squirm-inducing scene of the birth of a half human/half lizard.

THE SINGING DETECTIVE *(PBS; debuted Jan. 3, 1988)* This six-part serial from controversial playwright Dennis Potter ranks among the best-loved imports in the British pantheon (including *Upstairs, Downstairs*). The surreal (and, according to a U.K. tabloid, pornographic) tale centered on Philip Marlow, a miserable writer of pulpy detective novels who's bedridden due to psoriatic arthritis and tries to distract himself from the pain by mentally revising one of his novels, *The Singing Detective*. What results is like a drug-induced fever dream, as images of the crooning gumshoe's crime-fighting adventures mix with Marlow's frightening recollections of his painful wartime childhood. Here was proof positive that television could also be art.

LONESOME DOVE *(CBS; debuted Feb. 5, 1989)* Just when the world thought good Westerns had gone the way of silver spurs, Larry McMurtry's hugely popular (and Pulitzer Prize-winning) novel became an eight-hour shoot-'em-up showcase for Robert Duvall, as the low-key cowboy Augustus McCrae, and Tommy Lee Jones, as the laconic, upstanding Capt. Woodrow F. Call. The pair galloped across the open plains, rustling cattle, tussling with Indians, and reconnecting with their past: McCrae searched for his lost love, Clara Allen (Anjelica Huston), while Call came to terms with Newt Dobbs (Ricky Schroder), the lonely son he barely knew. Seven Emmys and one Peabody award later, *Lonesome Dove* had put the cowboy back in the Hollywood saddle.

ARMISTEAD MAUPIN'S TALES OF THE CITY (PBS; debuted Jan. 10, 1994) Three years before Ellen Morgan's outing, this serialized version of Maupin's quirky *San Francisco Chronicle* columns was earning notice—and a little notoriety—for its own televised portrayals of homosexuality. Set in 1976, *Tales* was an honest, funny, and provocative look at the culture of sex and love in the Bay City before AIDS arrived on the scene. It followed the residents of 28 Barbary Lane, including lovelorn Michael Tolliver (Marcus D'Amico), who just wanted to find the perfect man; fresh-faced Ohio native Mary Ann Singleton (Laura Linney), struggling to adjust to the big city; and landlady Anna Madrigal (Olympia Dukakis), a font of flighty wisdom. *Tales* had it all—drug use, drag queens, nudity—but it was the kiss between Michael and boyfriend Jon Fielden (William Campbell) that ignited the most controversy (some PBS affiliates refused to air it; others broadcast an edited version). Even so, by shedding light on America's ever-changing society, Maupin's motley cast of characters managed to achieve what so many great miniseries do: break new ground.

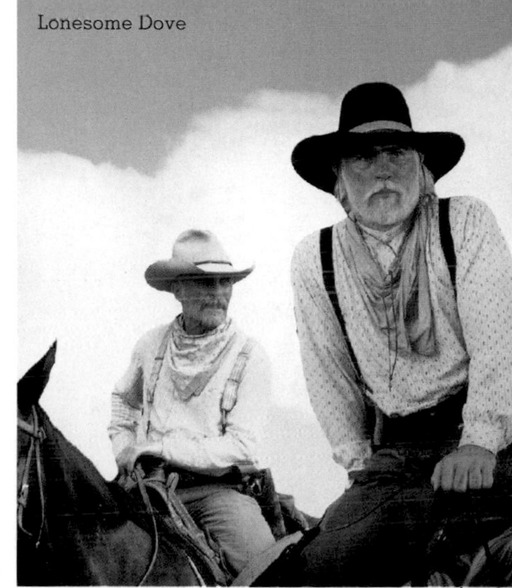
Lonesome Dove

ALK/

VARIETY

THE VARIETY FORMAT WAS WHERE TELEVISION FINALLY PROVED that it could do something not just better than any other medium, but differently. Is it any coincidence that the show that finally put the TV set over as a consumerist object of desire was Milton Berle's late-'40s *Texaco Star Theater*? Sketch comedy had long been a staple of radio, of course, but you had to see Uncle Miltie running around in a dress to get the gag. Ironically, the renaissance in TV variety also represented the last hurrah for old-time vaudeville: Not only was the emphasis on visual comedy punctuated by musical numbers and novelty acts, but many of the groundbreaking stars were rooted in the Broadway–Borscht Belt axis, and a lot of the routines were...let's just say well tested. ✦ And, as in vaudeville, there was a hierarchy. The more raucous shows like *Texaco* were pure, cheap-seats-and-baggy-pants buffoonery, while to appear on *The Ed Sullivan Show* (see the Top 20) was like playing the Palace. In the middle—and probably the finest, funniest, and most influential comedy-variety show in the history of television—was *Your Show of Shows*, which married brute slapstick to a sardonic, anarchic, modern silliness. ✦ Sid Caesar and company never messed with the underlying conventions of comedy, though—never really knocked down the walls and built a new house. That task fell to the wild man of video, Ernie Kovacs, who lurched out of Philadelphia in the early '50s with a comic style so confrontational and surreal (the Nairobi Trio? What was that about?) as to thoroughly defy imitation. ✦ Still, Caesar perfected the fundamentals and Kovacs reconnoitered the fringes, and between them they influenced almost all the comedy-variety shows that mattered. *Rowan & Martin's Laugh-In* smoothed out and sped up Kovacs' patented dementia and dressed it in bell-bottoms just in time for the late '60s. The show also introduced the notion of the large ensemble cast of farceurs, a concept *Saturday Night Live* would hone in the 1970s. *SNL*'s lengthy sketches, talented stable of writers, and musical guests owed something to Caesar and *Show of Shows*, but the air of aggressive comic danger felt like Kovacs reborn, and the show's success paved the way for Ernie's true modern heir, David Letterman. ✦ Somewhere along the way, though, the classic variety show dried up as a valid format and cultural force. Ed Sullivan died, the rock generation grew up, the TV landscape splintered into hundreds of specialty channels. To watch *SNL* at the turn of the millennium is, let's face it, more an exercise in willful pop nostalgia than a chance to see great, groundbreaking comedy. The genre, instead, has merged with the talk show and mutated into a daytime Circus Maximus, of which Oprah is undisputed queen and Jerry Springer the current clown. Variety used to be the spice of life. These days, life is the spice of variety. —TY BURR

PHOTOGRAPH BY NOLA LÓPEZ

SATURDAY NIGHT LIVE

STAYING HOME ON A WEEKEND NIGHT WAS NO LAUGHING MATTER—UNTIL 'SNL'

THERE WAS A TIME when no one under 25 would have been caught dead in front of the TV set come 11:30 Saturday night—wouldn't any self-respecting party animal be out carousing? That all changed in 1975 when NBC asked a 30-year-old producer named Lorne Michaels to create a show for the sex, drugs, and rock & roll generation. Suddenly the living-room couch became the place to be. ✦ Slamming late-night programming from snooze to alarm setting, Michaels pulled together a rogues' gallery of comics (mostly from Chicago's Second City and L.A.'s Groundlings groups), lined up weekly rock acts and celebrity hosts (NBC insisted that the first one, George Carlin, wear a suit with a T-shirt instead of jeans)—and the Not Ready for Prime Time Players were off and running. Nothing was sacred: Chevy Chase as a stumbling, bumbling President Ford; Dan Aykroyd and Jane Curtin as coneheaded aliens ("We are from France"); Gilda Radner as Emily Litella ("What's all this fuss about violins on TV?"); Bill Murray as Nick the Lounge Singer ("*Star Wars*/ Nothing but *Star Wars*..."); and John Belushi as—well, take your pick: Joe Cocker, a journeyman samurai, or a cranky bee. ✦ Over the years, the names have changed: Comedians from Eddie Murphy ("I'm Gumby, dammit!") and Mike Myers ("Not!") to Dana "Church Lady" Carvey have mugged and joked their way across *SNL*'s hallowed stage—and more than a few times, critics have driven a stake through the show's heart, proclaiming it *Saturday Night Dead*. But even after nearly a quarter century on the air, the show always manages to crawl back to cooldom. Though its wild youth is long gone, it's still *Saturday Night Live*—and you're not.

—JOE NEUMAIER/PHOTOGRAPH BY EDIE BASKIN

JUST THE FACTS

SATURDAY NIGHT LIVE

YEARS ON AIR 1975–present

TOP NIELSEN CHARTING Not available

EMMYS WON 14

ORIGINAL TITLE *Saturday Night.* The word *Live* was added to the title after a flop ABC variety series called *Saturday Night Live With Howard Cosell* was canceled.

FINE-TUNING THE CONCEPT Early on, the Muppets and short films by Albert Brooks were regular features. Neither made it past the first season.

PRESCIENT CASTING Billy Crystal was set to appear on the first show, but was bumped when his manager and agent argued with Michaels over the amount of time allotted to one of Crystal's sketches. He ended up joining the cast in 1984.

WOMEN'S ISSUES Belushi reportedly urged that all the show's female writers be fired, and once locked himself in his dressing room rather than perform in a skit written by a woman.

COMITY IS HARD After Chevy Chase left, he returned as a guest host and reportedly got into a fistfight with Bill Murray, who yelled, "This is my show now!"

WHAT MIGHT HAVE BEEN Shortly before John Lennon's death, he said he and Paul McCartney had been watching *SNL* in Lennon's New York City apartment when Michaels appeared on air and jokingly repeated an offer of $3,000 to the Beatles to reunite for one show. The two thought about showing up at the studio, but decided not to—"we were actually too tired," Lennon said.

WHAT DID THEY KNOW? In an early review, *The New York Times* wrote that "quality is an ingredient conspicuously absent from the dreadfully uneven comedy efforts of the new series."

JUST THE FACTS

THE CAROL BURNETT SHOW

YEARS ON AIR 1967–78

TOP NIELSEN CHARTING 13th (1969–70)

EMMYS WON 25

WHAT'S IN A NAME? Carol Burnett was named after Carole Lombard, her mother's favorite actress.

BEHIND THE LAUGHTER Later in life, Burnett revealed that the source of much of her working-class comedy was a childhood marked by difficult poverty and emotional abuse. Her escape was the movies; she sometimes saw eight in one week.

EARS TO YOU Burnett's trademark gesture of tugging on her ear was a way of saying hello to her adoring grandmother, who'd raised her.

IT BEATS WORKING AT THE SUPERMARKET Vicki Lawrence was cast as a regular in the show right out of high school, largely on the strength of her resemblance to Burnett.

ROWAN & MARTIN'S LAUGH-IN

YEARS ON AIR 1968–73

TOP NIELSEN CHARTING 1st (1968–69; 1969–70)

EMMYS WON 3

WHERE THEY GOT THE NAME *Laugh-In* refers to the late-'60s hippie catchphrase *love-in*.

WHERE THE IDEA WENT Lorne Michaels was a *Laugh-In* writer and launched *Saturday Night Live* two years after *Laugh-In* went off the air.

RIGHT-WING ROLE CALL For a putatively anti-establishment show, *Laugh-In* had some surprising guest stars: Billy Graham, Martha Mitchell, John Wayne, and William F. Buckley Jr.

WHY NIXON? *Laugh-In*'s head writer, Paul Keyes, was a friend of (and ex-speechwriter for) Richard Nixon.

DARING FOR ITS DAY "You know, we only went into Vietnam as advisers," Rowan quipped. "Last week, we dropped over 40,000 tons of advice."

THE CAROL BURNETT SHOW

THE WOMAN OF A THOUSAND FACES RAISED GOOFINESS TO A HIGH ART

MAYBE IT'S SOMETHING ABOUT the red hair. Like fellow carrottop Lucille Ball, Carol Burnett was her generation's queen of comedy, and every week from 1967 to 1978 on her eponymous CBS variety show, she proved herself worthy of the throne. Pratfalling, slow-burning, yodeling like Tarzan, Burnett clowned tirelessly alongside crazy cronies Lyle Waggoner, Harvey Korman, Vicki Lawrence, and Tim Conway (plus, in later stints, Ken Berry, Steve Lawrence, and Dick Van Dyke). ✦ Even now, the sketches' sublime silliness lingers: the overwrought faux soap *As the Stomach Turns*; Burnett and Conway as inept secretary Mrs. Wiggins and her long-suffering employer, Mr. Tudball; Korman and Burnett playing the endlessly bickering Ed and Eunice; a *Gone With the Wind* spoof in which Burnett's

Scarlett O'Hara makes her dress from drapes—complete with curtain rod. ✦ So what if Burnett and Co. kept dissolving into giggles at their own gags? Can you blame them? Everyone from Carol on down seemed to be having just as good a time as the audience was. From the unpretentiously friendly way she answered audience questions at the start of every show to her trademark earlobe tug at the end of the hour, the comedian's warmth infused every song and sketch. No wonder that during its 11-season run—one of the longest variety-show stints in history—*The Carol Burnett Show* won 25 Emmys. Well before "family entertainment" became a TV cliché, she created exactly that for more than a decade—and every week, she left us so glad we'd had this time together. —CAREN WEINER

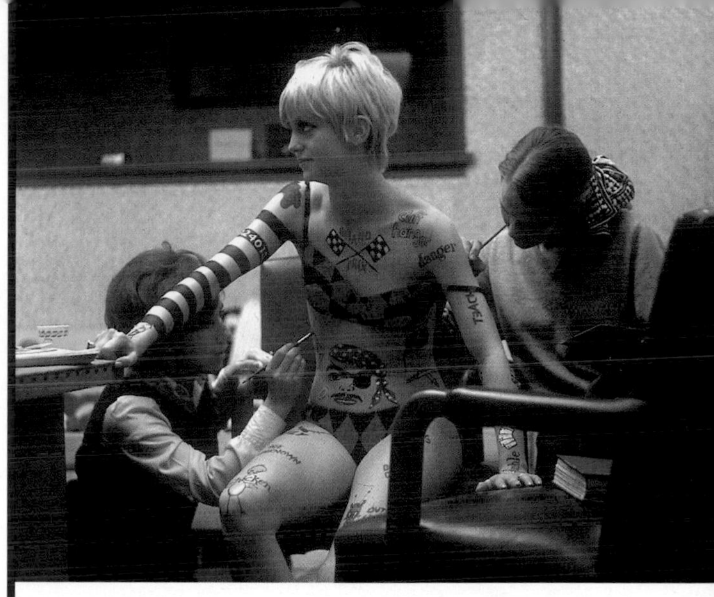

WHAT A LOVE-IN WE HAD WITH THIS ZANY GROOVEFEST

FROM "SOCK IT TO ME!" and "Here comes de judge" to Goldie Hawn's shimmying go-go girl and Ruth Buzzi's little old lady whacking dirty old men with her umbrella, *Rowan & Martin's Laugh In* provided the late '60s and early '70s with a lexicon of zany pop-culture catchphrases and sight gags. Producer George Schlatter persuaded NBC to put *Laugh-In* on the air, even though the network didn't expect much of it; the comedy-variety show (a mid-season replacement for *The Man From U.N.C.L.E.*) seemed destined to be cannon fodder against ratings powerhouses like *Gunsmoke*. But in a time of student protests and urban riots, perhaps America was weary of such bland fare as *The Andy Griffith Show* (1967's No. 1). And *Laugh-In*, hosted by Dan Rowan and Dick Martin and featuring such regulars as Hawn, Buzzi, Lily Tomlin, Arte Johnson, Judy Carne, and Henry Gibson, was anything but bland. With kaleidoscopic graphics and split-second pacing (the show positively flew through wacky sketches, punny one-liners, and surprise cameos—like John Wayne as the Easter Bunny), *Laugh-In* went about as far out as '60s TV dared. (It also occasionally smuggled a drug joke past the censors: A man walks up to Carne in a park and says, "Hi." Her reply: "You, too?") ✦ Even that most establishment of figures, Richard Nixon, jumped on the *Laugh-In* bandwagon. Schlatter believes that Nixon's "Sock it to *me*?" cameo (it took him five takes to nail it...sort of) helped him lock up enough youth votes to win the 1968 presidency. Who knows—maybe Nixon inspired another political figure, Bill Clinton, to blow his saxophone on *The Arsenio Hall Show* 24 years later. As Arte Johnson would mutter from behind his potted plant, "Verrrry interesting." —MATTHEW McCANN FENTON

ROWAN & MARTIN'S LAUGH-IN

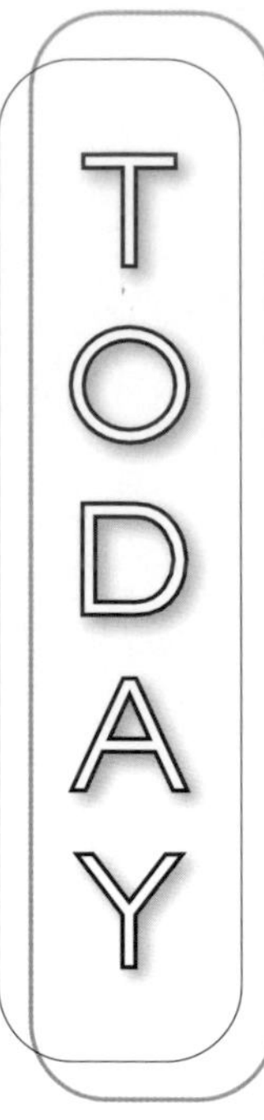

"WELL, HERE WE ARE, and good morning to you.... NBC begins a new program called *Today.* And if it doesn't sound too revolutionary, I really believe this begins a new kind of television." Thus spake easygoing host Dave Garroway on Jan. 14, 1952, more than 12,000 shows ago. It was a bold prediction—and a true one. ✦ Conceived by Peacock exec Pat Weaver (Sigourney's dad), the *Today* show did nothing less than change America's TV habits. No longer just an after-work treat, the tube became as integral to our mornings as hot showers. Just as important, the show kicked off a TV genre that is still spreading today: infotainment. ✦ The two-hour New York-based broadcast was the first to so skillfully—and brazenly—mix the heavy and the fluffy: interviews with everyone from Golda Meir to Robin Williams. Gene Shalit's cascade of atrocious puns. Bryant Gumbel's emotional visit to Africa. Muffin-baking segments with Martha Stewart. A live kidney transplant. Even the antics of a diaper-clad chimp named J. Fred Muggs, the show's mascot back in the early days. ✦ The talking heads may change—Hugh Downs, Jane Pauley, Tom Brokaw, Barbara Walters, Katie Couric, and Matt Lauer have all been our breakfast companions—but the show's split personality remains. Once in a while, the cracks appear: Remember the leaked 1989 memo in which Gumbel accused wacky weatherman Willard Scott of holding "the show hostage to his assortment of whims, wishes, birthdays, and bad taste"? But no matter. Most mornings, the *Today* show tastes as good as a coffee with two sugars. —A.J. JACOBS/PHOTOGRAPH BY PHILIPPE HALSMAN

THIS INFOTAINMENT COMBO PLATTER BECAME A BREAKFAST STAPLE

YOUR SHOW OF SHOWS

THE 'SNL' PRECURSOR POURED ON THE LATE-NIGHT LUNACY

FOR A WHILE, CAESAR RULED. As de facto emperor of the early-'50s NBC variety series *Your Show of Shows* (his empress was Imogene Coca), Sid Caesar presided over what is arguably the most influential early comedy on TV. ✦ He was backed up by a writing team that was the comedy equivalent of the '27 Yankees. The lineup, including Mel Brooks, Neil Simon, and later Carl Reiner, worked at a grueling pace—fueled, Caesar once said, by "a diet of electricity and hate" and by their desire to impress the notoriously demanding star. (When Caesar didn't like an idea, he'd pretend to machine-gun it in midair, complete with sound effects.) ✦ The result? Twenty-five years before *Saturday Night Live*, Caesar and Coca were doing it first, presenting a fast-paced, 90-minute mishmash of live skits (the husband-and-wife Hickenloopers, storyteller Somerset Winterset), film parodies (*From Here to Obscurity*), and guest-star routines. And let's not forget Caesar's forte: ad-libbing. Whether forgetting the names of guests, wearing the wrong costume, or rewriting a skit mid-performance, the master of live TV seamlessly translated gaffes into guffaws. ✦ As another Caesar learned, however, all fame is fleeting. After four years, the show was beginning to lose its freshness, and the three principals (Caesar, Coca, and producer Max Liebman) wanted to work independently. In 1954, *Your Show of Shows* left the air. Coca went on to a half-hour sitcom that lasted but a season; her costar headlined *Caesar's Hour*, which, though successful, never recaptured the glory of *Your Show of Shows.* The emperor's reign was at an end. —MMF/PHOTOGRAPH BY LEONARD MCCOMBE

JUST THE FACTS

TODAY

YEARS ON AIR 1952–present

TOP NIELSEN CHARTING Not available

EMMYS WON 13

ORIGINAL TITLE *The Rise and Shine Revue*

WHERE THEY GOT THE IDEA Ernie Kovacs' Philadelphia morning show proved there was an a.m. audience. NBC took the concept mainstream by enlisting onetime radio personality Garroway as *Today's* first host.

MIRANDA WARNINGS Weatherman Scott, who had previously worked as Bozo the Clown, once delivered the weather in a bizarre form of drag–dressed as Carmen Miranda.

PRESCIENT HIRING Walters' "*Today* girl" slot was variously held by Lee Meriwether and Florence Henderson, among others.

YOUR SHOW OF SHOWS

YEARS ON AIR 1950–54

TOP NIELSEN CHARTING 3rd (1950–51)

EMMYS WON 4

HORSING AROUND Caesar, who was known for his great physical strength, once knocked out with one punch a horse that had thrown his wife. (Years later, Mel Brooks wrote this into *Blazing Saddles*.) Caesar also punched holes in the office walls when the strain became too much.

OUR MR. BROOKS Caesar and Liebman disagreed over hiring the young Brooks. Caesar thought him funny; Liebman hated him. Caesar compromised by paying Brooks out of his own pocket–$40 a week.

MAD SCIENTIST One of the show's biggest fans was Albert Einstein, who loved Caesar's characterization of a know-it-all German professor. Einstein's secretary contacted Caesar to ask for a meeting, but the physicist died before it could take place.

JUST THE FACTS

THE LATE SHOW WITH DAVID LETTERMAN

YEARS ON AIR 1982–1992 (NBC); 1992–present (CBS)

TOP NIELSEN CHARTING Not available

EMMYS WON 7

PREVIOUS CAREER HIGHLIGHTS During his early career as a weatherman, Letterman once announced that Indianapolis was being pelted by "hailstones the size of canned hams." When reporting that a tropical storm had been upgraded to hurricane status, he congratulated the storm on its promotion.

SELF-ESTEEM ISSUES Letterman has called himself a "dweeb" and a "gap-toothed monkey boy," but objected that his portrayal in the HBO movie *The Late Shift* made him look like "a circus chimp" and "a budding psychopath."

WOMEN'S ISSUES Letterman has inspired female guests to call him an "a--hole" (Cher), contemplate smacking him (Shirley MacLaine), and use the F-word 13 times (Madonna).

SCTV NETWORK

YEARS ON AIR 1981–83

TOP NIELSEN CHARTING Not available

EMMYS WON 2

MAPLE LEAF RAG The Great White North sketches originated to satisfy the Canadian-content regulations of the CBC.

PEARLS BEFORE SWINE Dave Thomas once showed a tape of the "Play It Again, Bob" sketch to Bob Hope, whose only response was "Hey, you got the voice."

NONDISTINGUISHED PROGENY *SCTV* sometimes parodied the success of *SNL* with a format that featured a guest host (regular character Earl Camembert, played by Eugene Levy), a wildly pumped-up studio audience, and unfunny references to drugs.

NO THANKS In 1981, cast member Catherine O'Hara was asked to join the *SNL* cast; she returned to *SCTV* after just one week.

THE LATE SHOW WITH DAVID LETTERMAN

A CRANKY PRANKSTER WHO MAKES TALK HIP

A GAP-TOOTHED INDIANAPOLIS weatherman/comedian in thrall to Johnny Carson, Letterman set his sights on a talk show early on in his career. After he hosted a short-lived but frequently hilarious daytime talker in 1980 that allowed him to forge his trademark irreverent style, NBC in 1982 gave Letterman a new show with the plummiest of slots: 12:30 a.m., right after Carson. *Late Night With David Letterman* quickly developed a strong following among the young and the hip with such stunts as "Stupid Pet Tricks," "Top Ten" lists, and the "Monkey-cam," as well as such personalities as laid-back bandleader Paul Shaffer and the unnerving Larry "Bud" Melman. Letterman's ultimate goal was to replace Carson, but when NBC, fearing he was too edgy for the 11:30 slot, handed *The Tonight Show* to Jay Leno in 1992, a peeved Letterman accepted an offer from CBS to host *The Late Show With David Letterman*. ✦ In his new home, the host is still the bridge between old-fashioned talk-show style (you can see the influence of Steve Allen and Ernie Kovacs as well as Carson in his wacky yet good-hearted humor) and the more ironic, smart-alecky style that has since yielded *Late Night With Conan O'Brien* and Comedy Central's *The Daily Show*. Where Leno has gone for much broader humor, sometimes veering into crudity to boost his ratings, Letterman has stayed smart and unpredictable. Prickly, brooding, sometimes openly cranky he may be, but he's still the most interesting—and the most human—talk host of his generation. —KT

WE RAISE A TOAST TO THIS CANADIAN CLUB

HOW IRONIC IS IT that it took a bunch of Canadians to fashion a bull's-eye critique of '80s American pop culture? But that's just what *SCTV Network* did for two glorious seasons on NBC. ✦ Not content to heave mere satiric spitballs, the Second City comedy troupe created an entire ersatz TV network, based in the fictional town of Melonville. Its roster of shows-within-the-show ran the gamut from scary-movie anthologies ("Monster Chiller Horror Theater: Dr. Tongue's 3-D House of Stewardesses") to soaps ("The Days of the Week") to talk shows ("The Sammy Maudlin Show"). ✦ More important, though, its fourth-wall-breaking conceit put the very idea of celebrity under a microscope. It laid bare the raging egos and petty vendettas of its sprawling cast of characters, a ball that *The Larry Sanders Show* would take and run with nearly a decade later. ✦ In the process, *SCTV* established a slew of real and fabricated careers, like Joe Flaherty's sleazoid station owner, Guy Caballero; John Candy's blustering raconteur, Johnny LaRue; Andrea Martin's leopard-clad battle-ax, Edith Prickley; Martin Short's Ed Grimley; and Dave Thomas and Rick Moranis' beer-addled McKenzie brothers. ✦ But behind the nonstop hilarity, *SCTV*'s subtext seemed to be, Fame is cheap and getting cheaper, while the public's craving for it knows no bounds. Looking back in our collective rearview mirror at Jim and Tammy Faye Bakker, Kato Kaelin, and Joey Buttafuoco, it's shocking to see how prophetic these jokers were. —MIKE FLAHERTY

THE OPRAH WINFREY SHOW

YOU MAY HAVE LOST WEIGHT, come out of the closet, or confronted childhood abuse in these sensitive New Age '90s, but you haven't really felt your pain till you've worked it through on *The Oprah Winfrey Show.* ✦ What began as a local morning-chat gig in Baltimore in 1984 has become a virtual community of 14 million members and a cultural metaphor of truly apple-pie proportions: *Oprah* is sharing, caring, crying, hugging, commiserating. Meanwhile, she's become smaller, tauter, leaner (look, honey, she brought it up first, lugging 67 symbolic pounds of shed fat onto the set in 1988), more in control. ✦ Walking—make that *power* walking—the finest of lines between absolute empathy and total command, Winfrey redefined the talk show, out-*Donahue*ing Donahue with her relentless mike sharing and steady audience patrol. Then, when a host of Rickis and Sallys and Montels sprung up behind her, she redefined the genre again, publicly vowing to throw her sway only behind "messages of hope and possibility." Who else but Oprah could sandwich tea-sipping book-club meetings—which propel her handpicked literary selections to bestsellerdom—between segments on spirituality and racism, chats with her personal trainer, and a parade of highly coveted celebrity guests? If Madonna or Michael Jackson or J.F.K. Jr. have something to say and want people to hear it, they take it to the Chicago superwoman. Of course, she can also boogie with an of-the-moment pop group like Hanson, dispense viewer favors like Halloween candy—and still yak about junk food. ✦ She's your girlfriend, your confidante, your teacher—your sound-bite shrink on a national couch. —ALEXANDRA JACOBS/PHOTOGRAPH BY CHARLES BENNETT

FEELING FAT? LOOKING FOR A SPIRITUAL LIFT? NEED A GOOD BOOK? SHE'S YOUR GAL.

THE ERNIE KOVACS SHO

THE IMPORTANCE OF BEING ERNIE: COMEDY OWES A LOT TO THE MUSTACHIOED MAESTRO OF MAYHEM

IF YOU COULD SET A TIME machine to find the true father of David Letterman and other recent comedy innovators, you'd probably wind up in the greasy mustache of Ernie Kovacs. The loose-limbed, cigar-wielding creator of the 1950s' most mischievous variety show had a vision that was so far ahead of his early-TV contemporaries, it only gets clearer with age. ✦ In two separate runs of *The Ernie Kovacs Show* (as well as various specials and such shows as *Ernie in Kovacsland* and *Kovacs Unlimited*), the former DJ and sportscaster threw convention out the door, pioneering the use of rapid-fire, one-after-the-next skits and quirky visual effects (like musical kitchenware), all the while maintaining the loosest possible affiliation with reality. Some bits resembled an offbeat Charles Addams cartoon come to life; others were running gags featuring buffoonish characters like the speech-impaired poet Percy Dovetonsils or the German disc jockey Wolfgang Sauerbraten. And no topic was off limits: Kovacs wittily spoofed sponsors, movies, even TV itself, all the while holding court with that ever-present cigar jammed in his maw. ✦ He was self-mocking, hilarious, and cool as a cucumber—and if he smoked a Cuban cigar on the air, well, that was just part of being Ernie (Kovacs died at age 42 in a car crash as he was reaching for yet another cigar). In *Kovacsland*, the funniest thing you could do was to laugh at yourself—and the host was the master of putting himself in his own crosshairs. —JN

JUST THE FACTS

THE OPRAH WINFREY SHOW

YEARS ON AIR 1986–present

TOP NIELSEN CHARTING Not available

EMMYS WON 16

WHERE SHE'S FROM Oprah spent the first six years of her life on a pig farm in Kosciusko, Miss.

WHAT'S IN A NAME? Oprah is a misspelling of the biblical name Orphah. Winfrey's production company, Harpo, uses her name spelled backward.

TOUGH BREAKS At age 13, Oprah was sent to a juvenile home but was turned away due to overcrowding. At age 14, she gave birth to a premature baby who died. She later said the child might have been fathered by an uncle who had abused her.

SURPRISE! She once gave her best friend, fellow talk-show host Gayle King, a Christmas present of $1.25 million.

THE ERNIE KOVACS SHOW

YEARS ON AIR 1952–53, 1956

TOP NIELSEN CHARTING Not available

EMMYS WON 1

LATER CAREER HIGHLIGHT On Jan. 19, 1957, Kovacs hosted *The Silent Show*, the first prime-time network show done entirely in pantomime.

WHERE HE GOT THE ENERGY Kovacs said that he maintained his pace with "three steam baths a day, lots of good brandy, about 20 cigars, and work all night."

THE END Kovacs died in 1962 after his Corvair skidded out on a wet Santa Monica Boulevard and hit a utility pole. He had just attended a party celebrating Milton and Ruth Berle's adoption of a baby boy. His motto is etched on his tombstone: "Nothing in Moderation."

IN HIS ENGAGING, closely argued defense of TV, *Teleliteracy*, David Bianculli writes that "rejecting the entire medium of television on the basis of *Charlie's Angels* is no more logical than rejecting the entire motion-picture industry on the basis of *Porky's*." ✦ Man, even *he* doesn't get it. Television is a wondrous thing *because* of *Charlie's Angels*, not in spite of it. The TV shows highlighted in this chapter represent the crassest possible responses to the cultural needs of their eras, and, as such, they are both ridiculous and necessary. They're also fun; in fact, they're nothing else but fun. That's why, like a completely unredeeming tiramisu, they're irresistible. Admit it: You flipped to this chapter first, didn't you? It's okay, you don't have to eat your vegetables. ✦ Some Guilty Pleasures are just dumbed-down versions of existing genres married to the most frivolous of high-concept ideas. *Swiss Family Robinson* + rocket ships = *Lost in Space*. Cops + hippies = *The Mod Squad*. Detectives + T&A = *Charlie's Angels*. You get the idea, and we all have our private, rarely divulged favorite (okay, I'll cop: Man + deceased parent reincarnated as 1928 Porter = *My Mother the Car*). Other shows just plonk an ensemble of characters (make it a family if you're feeling really lazy) into a fish-out-of-water setting. Hillbillies in Hollywood. Monsters in suburbia. Gilligan, the Skipper too, a millionaire and his wife, a movie star, the Professor and Mary Ann on a deserted island. You don't need a Ph.D. to think this stuff up. ✦ The best of Guilty Pleasures are the ones that resonate with meaning in spite of their ineffable dumbness. Who'd have thought that *The Brady Bunch* would become a touchstone of kitschy functional-family innocence? (Even its late star, Robert Reed, once said about the show, "It was just as inconsequential as can be. I do not want it on my tombstone." Sorry, Bob.) Who knew that *Happy Days*, a show about the '50s, would now serve as a pungent time capsule of the '70s? ✦ Of course, it's much harder to create a Guilty Pleasure on purpose. Irony and whimsy both curdle when they're too thought-out, as even stalwart fans of a show like *Northern Exposure* will have to admit. The playful *Batman* was the rare series to pull off intentional idiocy, and that had a lot to do with its Pop-art times. ✦ The current Guilty Pleasures trend is toward preposterous dramas like *Beverly Hills 90210* and *Melrose Place*, both shows that can annoy when they cater to camp and are much more fun when they play it straight. As long as they make it easy for us to hate them, we'll love them. And something more: As the real world gets weirder and darker and faster, we need them. How else do you explain the fact that in the weeks following John F. Kennedy's assassination, the nation turned en masse to...*The Beverly Hillbillies*? Guilty Pleasures are candy, to be sure—but they'll do as painkillers in a pinch. —TY BURR

PHOTOGRAPH BY NOLA LÓPEZ

GUILTY PLEASURES

CHARLIE'S ANGELS

FANS OF THIS SHOW fall into two categories—those who view it as a feminist affirmation, proof that women can solve crimes just like the guys. (Somewhere in the world, there must be at least a half-dozen people in that group.) And the rest of us, who see the ABC series for what it really was: the ultimate guilty pleasure, a jiggle show that so prized style over substance you could enjoy it just as much (maybe even *more*) with the sound turned off. ✦ The fairy-tale tone of this Aaron Spelling creation was summed up in the opening voice-over: "Once upon a time, there were three little girls who went to the police academy...." The putative purpose of this small harem of private detectives (working for a never-seen boss named Charlie who literally phoned in his lines) was to sniff out bad guys. But what the Angels *really* did was provide for equal-opportunity ogling: For those who liked intellectual types, there was Kate Jackson as brainy Sabrina; for those who preferred cool beauties, there was Jaclyn Smith as ex-showgirl Kelly; and for practically every adolescent boy in the Western Hemisphere (and a few of their dads, too, peeking out from behind their papers), there was ex-Wella Balsam pitchbabe Farrah Fawcett-Majors, a sporty-looking blond who rode one mega-season on the show—and a kittenish swimsuit poster that left little to the imagination—to virtual cult status. (Asked for his theory on why Farrah's poster sold some 8 million copies, her then manager, Jay Bernstein, said, "Nipples.") ✦ Over the show's five-year run, the actresses playing the Angels changed with regularity (Fawcett was replaced by Cheryl Ladd, Jackson by Shelley Hack), but the plots remained predictable, always taking the Angels to places—women's prisons, health spas, casinos—where they could (a) masquerade as prostitutes, masseuses, or showgirls; (b) prance around in various states of undress; (c) somehow end up bound, gagged, or chained; and (d) utter such dramatic gems as "Freeze, turkey!" After five years, the stories started to wear as thin as Fawcett's maillot—and then it was halo, goodbye. —MATTHEW McCANN FENTON

✦ THESE SEXY WOMEN IN—AND OUT OF—UNIFORM LET MALE VIEWERS ENJOY AN HOUR OF ARRESTED DEVELOPMENT

CHARLIE'S ANGELS

YEARS ON AIR 1976–81

TOP NIELSEN CHARTING 4th (1977–78)

EMMYS WON 0

THE CAT'S MEOW The sho was first called *The Alley C* The name *Charlie's Angels* suggested by Jackson whe she saw a picture of a grou cherubim on Spelling's wall

ACTION JACKSON The sho was originally conceived as

for Jackson, who'd
ı the cop show
okies.

EL AT HIS TABLE 's original contract stip-
nat she be able to leave
each day in time
dinner for her then
d Lee Majors, star of
Million Dollar Man.

FLIGHT Because of
gation to *Charlie's*
Jackson was forced to
wn the role in *Kramer*
ner that eventually won
a Best Supporting Actress Oscar for Meryl Streep. Jackson left the show the following year.

CLOTHES ENCOUNTERS The average episode featured eight different outfits for each star.

TALKING HEAD The authoritative, deeply resonant voice of Charlie that came out of the speakerphone each week was provided by John Forsythe—who would go on to star in another Spelling show, *Dynasty.*

INVESTED INTEREST *Hart to Hart* star Robert Wagner and wife Natalie Wood were investors in the show; when producers Spelling and Leonard Goldberg explained the concept, Wagner labeled it "the worst idea I've ever heard."

WING-A-DING-DING The Fox network had plans to revive the series in 1988 (and call it, appropriately, *Angels '88*), but the new show (with four Angels this time, including Téa Leoni) never got off the ground.

JUSTTHEFACTS

LOST IN SPACE

YEARS ON AIR 1965–68

TOP NIELSEN CHARTING 35th (1965–66)

EMMYS WON 0

ARCHIE RIVAL The role of Dr. Smith was reportedly written for Carroll O'Connor (later of *All in the Family*), who turned it down.

GALAXY TUNES The theme was by John Williams, who later scored *Star Wars*.

YOU BET YOUR LIFE Allen's pal Groucho Marx was a primary investor in *LIS*.

IT'S LONELY IN OUTER SPACE... A scene in which Major West gives John Robinson mouth-to-mouth resuscitation was cut by censors, who feared kids would be unsettled by seeing two men's mouths touching.

...ESPECIALLY WHEN YOU CAN'T TOUCH YOUR WIFE For the same reason, censors ruled that the Robinson parents could have no physical contact.

GILLIGAN'S ISLAND

YEARS ON AIR 1964–67

TOP NIELSEN CHARTING 19th (1964–65)

EMMYS WON 0

MINNOW ROLES Early cast ideas were Raquel Welch for Mary Ann, Carroll O'Connor for the Skipper, and Jerry Van Dyke for Gilligan.

WILLIE BOY IS HERE Gilligan's first name was never revealed, but Schwartz and Denver thought he'd be a Willie.

WHAT'S IN A NAME The Skipper's real moniker [cut off] Jonas Grumby; the Pro[cut off] was Roy Hinkley.

SOS The U.S. Coast Gu[cut off] received telegrams fro[cut off] cerned citizens beggin[cut off] rescue of "those poor [cut off] before they starve to d[cut off]

CRITICS' LIPS COULDN'[cut off] SHIPS "It's difficult to be[cut off] *Gilligan's Island* was writ[cut off] directed, and filmed by a[cut off] said the *San Francisco* [cut off]

IN THIS '60S KITSCH-FEST, MORE THAN THE MOON WAS MADE OF CHEESE

IRWIN ALLEN, TV'S KING OF future schlock, may have brought us such camp classics as *Voyage to the Bottom of the Sea*, *The Time Tunnel*, and *Land of the Giants*, but he is probably best remembered for one of the cheesiest shows

LOST IN SPACE

ever to get off the ground, *Lost in Space*. The series came about because CBS wanted to cash in on public interest–especially among kids–in the space program by launching its own spaceship (one with children as part of the crew, to boot). ✦ The plot focused on a peripatetic brood, a Swiss Family Robinson for the space-conscious '60s (including, as the mom and dad, former TV Zorro Guy Williams and June Lockhart, who had traded in her Lassie shirtwaists for form-fitting silver astro-gear). The Robinsons took off on a five-year mission to the Alpha Centauri star system, only to find that their craft had been tampered with and that they were...well, lost. In space. (Along for the ride were the sniveling saboteur Dr. Zachary Smith and a bubbleheaded, accordion-armed robot famed for bellowing "Danger, Will Robinson!") ✦ Finally, here was a show that raised sub-par production values to high camp; in fact, *Lost in Space*'s healthier ratings were a bitter pill for the rival–and infinitely more serious–space series *Star Trek*. (You would never have seen giant vegetables attacking the *Enterprise* crew.) The result? A veritable vichyssoise of interstellar hoots. —MMF

IS THERE AN American alive who can't tell you what happened after "five passengers set sail that day on a three-hour tour"? Of course not–when the SS *Minnow* wrecked on an uncharted South Pacific island, the castaways (Gilligan, the Skipper, the Howells, Ginger, the Professor, and Mary Ann, as if you didn't know) spent 98 episodes screwing up every possible opportunity to be rescued from their uncharted desert isle. ✦ Sure, the entire concept of the CBS show was silly and illogical–if the Professor could rig up a bicycle-powered gramophone out of the few materials they had on the island, how come he couldn't manage to build a decent raft? But *Gilligan*'s fans were clearly unfazed by the show's broad-as-a-barn writing and slapstick routines (no matter how many times Alan Hale's Skipper laid a kick into the backside of Bob Denver's Gilligan, a sort of '60s Forrest Gump). To its creator, Sherwood Schwartz, Gilligan's lowbrow appeal was inevitable–Schwartz started out with a highfalutin concept in which the passengers constituted a "social microcosm," then later admitted the castaways were really "more caricatures than characters." ✦ But so what? Their cartoonish antics entered the pantheon of great TV mysteries: How did Thurston Howell III get a year's supply of booze? Just where did Ginger and Mary Ann get all those clothes? And their two-dimensional status made it that much more likely that they would, say, gain superpowers by eating radioactive vegetables, or fend off misguided cosmonauts, or stage a musical version of *Hamlet* ("I ask to be, or not to be, and that is the question that I ask of me"). Castaways they may have been, but they were never cast down–and, watching them, neither were we. —CAREN WEINER

GILLIGAN'S ISLAND

THE SERIES' PREMISE COULDN'T HOLD WATER, BUT THIS CASTAWAY COMEDY WAS STILL SEE-WORTHY

BEVERLY HILLS 90210

TELEVISION HAS ALWAYS BEEN crammed with teenagers—either gee-whiz kids (Wally Cleaver) or smart-alecky wisenheimers (Alex P. Keaton) with blemish-free lives that never get more complex than "Gee, how can I find a date for the dance?" Then, in October 1990, Aaron Spelling, TV's foremost soap-meister, put forth his most ambitious creation yet: a show about adolescents with real-life problems. Sure, the residents of *Beverly Hills 90210* were an annoyingly beautiful bunch living in a fantasy zip code of upscale shopping malls and cool cars, but Brenda Walsh (Shannen Doherty) and her pals had concerns that would've made Joanie Cunningham blush: I want to have sex with my alcoholic boyfriend, but I'm too busy worrying about the lump in my breast. ✦ The sun-dappled Fox soap opera didn't catch on right away (programmed as it was opposite NBC's Thursday powerhouse, *Cheers*). In the summer of 1991, however, the upstart net grabbed vacationing teens by airing original episodes featuring the *90210* gang enjoying their summer vacations too. Instantly, eight teen idols—bitchy Brenda, brooding Dylan (Luke Perry), doltish Steve (Ian Ziering), goody-goody Brandon (Jason Priestley), spoiled Kelly (Jennie Garth), virginal Donna (Tori Spelling), Vanilla Ice wannabe David (Brian Austin Green), and brainy Andrea (Gabrielle Carteris)—were born. By deftly combining eternal themes of crushes and cliques with more topical messages about honorability and friendship, *90210* offered teens a modified mirror image of what being young in the '90s was all about. ✦ While the notoriously difficult Doherty exited in 1994 and the show's story lines eventually became more soapy and less earnest, the important things stayed the same: the gang's internal loyalty, the Peach Pit's menu, and, of course, Brandon's hair. —KRISTEN BALDWIN/PHOTOGRAPH BY MIKEL ROBERTS

TOO COOL FOR SCHOOL: THIS TEEN GANG MORE THAN MADE THE GRADE

GREASERS, SOCK HOPS, POODLE SKIRTS—THOSE WERE THE 'DAYS'

HAPPY DAYS

TO FIND A NORMAL FAMILY during the '70s, you had to go back to the '50s, when malt shops and hula hoops were king. In 1974, those *Happy Days* were here again, thanks to three kids named Richie, Potsie, and Ralph. ✦ The series began life as an episode of *Love, American Style*, but its pilot was shelved until, in a wonderful moment of kismet, Ron Howard starred in George Lucas' wildly popular *American Graffiti* (1973). Suddenly, the rage for the age of greasers was on, and ABC execs were only too happy to cash in. Yet again, Howard played a cardigan-sweatered good guy: His Richie Cunningham had the requisite sage dad (Tom Bosley), sweet-as-angel-food-cake mom (Marion Ross), and poodle-skirted kid sis Joanie (Erin Moran). Even better, he had a hood with a heart of gold living upstairs. And when the pompadoured, leather-jacketed Arthur "Fonzie" Fonzarelli (Henry Winkler) rode his big bike on screen, America cheered. (So popular did the cuddly James Dean wannabe become that execs even considered renaming the show *Fonzie's Happy Days*.) ✦ Still, it was his odd-couple friendship with the squeaky-clean Richie (protecting him from a gang of toughs or sharing some hard-earned wisdom about girls) that resonated with audiences—so much so that the coming-of-age show launched ABC's first big boom, featuring shows like *Three's Company* and *Days* spin-off *Laverne & Shirley*. As the Fonz would say, Heyyy, that's cool, Mr. C. —JOE NEUMAIER

LY HILLS 90210

ON AIR 1990–present

ELSEN CHARTING
994–95)

S WON 0

NAL TITLE *Class of*
y Hills

A CHAMELEON At the
ing of the second season,
y Hills, 90210 mysteriously
d the punctuation from its
d became *Beverly*
0210.

HOW IT ALL BEGAN Fox chairman Barry Diller called once-hot but by then lukewarm producer Aaron Spelling and asked, "Would you like to do something about a high school?"

WHAT DID THEY KNOW? *The Washington Post* accused the producers of creating "a vacuum, a perfect void, a black hole in the already vast and empty TV schedule."

SPIN-OFFS *Melrose Place*

HAPPY DAYS

YEARS ON AIR 1974–84

TOP NIELSEN CHARTING 1st (1976–77)

EMMYS WON 1

ORIGINAL TITLE The pilot was called *New Family In Town.*

FIFTIES VERITE Early episodes were photographed on film, produced without a laugh track, and shot mostly on location.

FINE-TUNING THE CONCEPT ABC wanted a whole gang of greasers added to the cast. Creator Garry Marshall compromised by writing in a single leather-jacketed biker–Fonzie.

WHAT'S IN A NAME? Fonzie was going to be called Marscharelli–Marshall's real name–but producers settled on Arthur Fonzarelli.

REVIVED TUNE Bill Haley's 1955 smash "Rock Around the Clock" became a hit record all over again thanks to its exposure on *Happy Days.*

JUSTTHEFACTS

THE MOD SQUAD

THIS TROIKA OF REBELS WITH A CAUSE WAS COP LAND'S LINK TO THE COUNTERCULTURE

THE BASIC IDEA for *The Mod Squad* had been kicking around since 1960, when former police officer Bud Ruskin wrote a pilot about three youths recruited to work as undercover cops. Maybe it was a good thing the show took so long to get on the air. By 1968, when the series, produced by Aaron Spelling, finally premiered on ABC, the counterculture was in full bloom, and the burgeoning hippie movement (Free love! Be-ins! Acid trips!) provided fodder for all sorts of story lines that would have been unimaginable a few years earlier. ✦ The Squad itself was a trio of young rebels, each of whom was given a second chance—and a cause—by LAPD captain Adam Greer (Tige Andrews) after running afoul of the law. The team was a study in contrasts: Linc Hayes (Clarence Williams III) was an angry, Afro-wearing black militant who'd been busted in the Watts riots; Pete Cochran (Michael Cole) came from Beverly Hills affluence but had rejected his parents' materialistic values and been arrested for car theft; and Julie Barnes (the luminous Peggy Lipton) was a prostitute's daughter who'd traded her unhappy home life for a vagrancy rap after running away. ✦ Each week, this unlikely hippie trio ferreted out dastardly adult criminals who sought to exploit righteously confused kids (although a good deal of the show's frisson was sparked by the simmering tensions among the three very different individuals). With its bell-bottoms and period slang, *The Mod Squad* was very much a show of its time, an obvious attempt to cash in on the never-trust-anyone-over-30 freak scene. Still, more than two decades after it went off the air in 1973, it retains a certain charm. Perhaps it wasn't so far-out, but it was still pretty groovy. —TOM SINCLAIR

HAWAII FIVE

RIPPLING WATERFALLS. Babes in bikinis. Gorgeous sunsets. Who would have guessed there could be trouble in this tropical paradise? Well, Jack Lord, for one, who, in his well-starched blue suit and perfect helmet of hair, literally lorded it over the islands as Steve McGarrett, the head of the elite Five-O crime-fighting branch of the Hawaii State Police. ✦ Of course, for many devotees, the real star of the show was the Wave, the tsunami that not only launched *Hawaii Five-O*'s stupendous opening-credit sequence—a fast-cut montage of beaches and bodies, pulsing to a theme song that rose to No. 4 on the *Billboard* charts in 1969—but also preceded each commercial break. But hit songs come and go; there had to be more of a reason for *Five-O*'s long reign on the tube. That reason: the implacable and incorruptible McGarrett, played by an actor whose behind-the-camera bossiness approached James Cameron dimensions. Lord reportedly bullied directors, told the crew how he should be lit, and refused to share any costarring credit, even with his longtime No. 2, Danny Williams (played with near constant befuddlement by James MacArthur). ✦ Viewed now, the CBS program serves as a fascinating mirror of the crime concerns obsessing America during the show's 1968–1980 run: Vietnam grunts gone wacko and flower children gone bad, Communist infiltrators, Mafia hitmen, and slimy pimps (one played by Gavin MacLeod!). The best episodes feature McGarrett's nemesis, "Red" Chinese mastermind Wo Fat (played by Khigh Dhiegh of *Manchurian Candidate* fame). But high or low, scuzzy or slick, none could outsmart Steve McGarrett. In those final seconds, he always busted his cases wide open, barking the words that sent a shiver down the spine of *Five-O* aficionados everywhere: "Book 'em, Danno." —NANCY BILYEAU

VIEWERS LEI'D THEIR TRUST IN STEVE McGARRETT TO MAKE THE 50TH STATE WO FAT-FREE

UAD

IR 1968–1973

N CHARTING 11th

0

EALITY *The Mod*
based on Ruskin's
in an undercover
by young cops
.

MOD WORLD
, who later married
cer Quincy Jones,

made an album in 1968 and cowrote the song "L.A. Is My Lady," which became the title track of Frank Sinatra's 1984 album.

ODD PLACE FOR A REUNION Lipton and Williams acted together again in a scene from David Lynch's series *Twin Peaks* (Lipton, a regular, played Norma Jennings, and Williams guest-starred for one episode).

STOP! IN THE NAME OF LOVE Williams and *Cagney & Lacey*'s Tyne Daly linked up in 1995.

HAWAII FIVE-O

YEARS ON AIR 1968–1980

TOP NIELSEN CHARTING 3rd (1972–73)

EMMYS WON 2

THE LONG ARM OF THE LAW *Five-O* is the longest-running cop show in TV history. (*Dragnet* ran for the same amount of time, but not continuously.)

BACKGROUND CHECK It was rumored that Lord altered his CBS biography and fudged his age. If the year given for his birth were accurate, Lord would have graduated from high school when he was 7.

ART IMITATES LIFE Walk-on parts for cops were often played by real Hawaiian police officers.

HIS LORDSHIP After the show ended, Lord reportedly considered running for governor of Hawaii.

BOOK THOSE FLIGHTS, DANNO The show so boosted Hawaiian tourism that the state now has an official Jack Lord Day.

JUST THE FACTS

BATMAN

YEARS ON AIR 1966–68

TOP NIELSEN CHARTING 5th (1965–66; mid-season replacement)

EMMYS WON 0

DYNAMIC DUO RATINGS *Batman*, one of very few network shows ever to appear on two different nights each week, is the only show to hold two spots in Nielsen's yearly top 10.

A REAL BOY WONDER Ward, who had a brown belt in karate, helped convince producers he was right for the role of Robin by breaking a brick with his bare hand at his audition.

CAPED CRUSADE *Batman* got a special commendation from the National Safety Council for showing the Dynamic Duo snapping on safety belts in the Batmobile.

A WILD JOKER Frank Sinatra wanted to play clown prince of crime the Joker, but Cesar Romero got the part.

HOLY CAREER CHANGE! Pierre Salinger, who'd previously been press secretary for President John F. Kennedy, played the villain Lucky Pierre.

THE LONE RANGER

YEARS ON AIR 1949–57

TOP NIELSEN CHARTING Never ranked in top 25

EMMYS WON 0

WHITE MAN'S BURDEN Writers were required to make sure the Ranger spoke with perfect grammar and never killed anyone, cursed, drank, smoke, gambled, or lusted.

AT HOME WITH THE RANGER In a case of voluntary typecasting, Moore continued to make appearances as the Lone Ranger long after the show had ended.

WHO WAS THAT MASKED MAN? Moore was ordered by a judge to stop appearing in public as the Lone Ranger after the Wrather Corp. (which owned the rights to the character) complained. Moore obeyed the order but continued to make appearances in dark wraparound sunglasses. In 1985, Wrather withdrew its complaint and Moore rode again.

BATMAN

LET THE PURIST DROOLERS drone on about how Tim Burton's films truly plumbed the depths of the Dark Knight's brooding soul—it was the 1966-68 ABC series that captured the comic book's spirit of fun. As the slightly paunchy Caped Crusader, Adam West fought Gotham City bad guys with a tongue-in-cheek glee. His sidekick, Robin (Burt Ward), exuded an infectiously boyish enthusiasm bordering on mania ("Holy contributing to the delinquency of minors, Batman!"). ✦ The show had it all: exciting action sequences (with evocative sound-effects phrases like "THWACK!" and "ZOWIE!" flashing up on the screen), nifty gadgets (the Batarang, the Batgeiger Counter), and guest stars galore. In addition to heinous villains like the Joker (Cesar Romero), the Penguin (Burgess Meredith), and the Riddler (Frank Gorshin), there were lesser, but no less kitschy, figures like "Fingers" Chandell (Liberace) and Lola Lasagne (Ethel Merman). As Meredith recalled, "After its first few episodes, *Batman* became the in thing to do." Celebrities from Jerry Lewis to Sammy Davis Jr. to Edward G. Robinson contributed cameos, popping out of windows as Batman and Robin scaled the sides of buildings. ✦ *Batman* was a fantasy in more ways than one: Many a prepubescent boy's dirty dreams were inspired by the formfitting costumes of the crime-busting Batgirl (Yvonne Craig) and the evil temptress Catwoman—who'll always be remembered as Julie Newmar, despite the fact that the female feline was also played by Lee Meriwether and Eartha Kitt. Not to mention Michelle What's-her-name. —BRUCE FRETTS/PHOTOGRAPH BY CURT GUNTHER

POW! THE COSTUMES! ZOOM! THE GUEST VILLAINS! BAM! THE CAMP! THIS COMIC-BOOK HERO WAS WAY OVER THE TOP (AND WHOLLY FUN).

THE LONE RANGER

YES, KEMO SABE, THAT MASKED MAN WAS ONE OF EARLY TV'S MOST POPULAR WHITE HATS

TO THE THUNDERING STRAINS of Rossini's "William Tell Overture," over images of a masked man astride a majestic white stallion, a narrator breathlessly spoke the words that thrilled a generation: "A fiery horse with the speed of light, a cloud of dust, and a hearty 'Hi-yo, Silver!'...the Lone Ranger rides again!" ✦ Actually, *The Lone Ranger* had been galloping into kids' hearts for decades: Original episodes aired on radio from 1933 to 1954; the show was so successful it became the cornerstone of an entire radio network, and on TV from 1949 to 1957, it marked the first bona fide hit for the fledgling American Broadcasting Co. No wonder. The hero's appeal was as timeless as that of Robin Hood and Zorro, similarly larger-than-life characters with a hint of mystery about them. ✦ The series, which followed the Western adventures of a do-gooder former Texas Ranger, may have been kid stuff but it was also loaded with adult-friendly messages: The Ranger (Clayton Moore) was best friends with an Indian (Jay Silverheels' Tonto) long before it was fashionable, he always shot to wound (never to kill), and he was so morally upright he even got the endorsement of J. Edgar Hoover. The show had its appealingly operatic touches, too: A silver bullet was the hero's calling card, while his mask was meant to strike fear into the hearts of his foes. Still, this Ranger was modest, riding anonymously off as soon as a job was complete. "Who was that masked man?" his beneficiaries would ask. Who indeed? A true American folk hero. —TOM SOTER

DYNASTY

BAD TASTE, MORE FILLING: FOR THIS 'DALLAS'-WANNABE, NOTHING SUCCEEDED LIKE EXCESS

RUTHLESS TYCOONS, trust-fund hussies, mergers gone bad, and the most tastelessly lavish decor since Marie Antoinette redecorated the Petit Trianon—yep, if any show personified the delectably decadent 1980s, it was *Dynasty*. ✦ It all began when ABC, covetous of CBS' cash cow, *Dallas*, created its own moguls-behaving-badly soap in 1981, casting leonine John Forsythe as new-money gazillionaire Blake Carrington and big-shouldered Linda Evans as his secretary-turned-wife, Krystle, living not so happily ever after in Denver. ✦ At first, the ratings well came up dry, so executive producer Aaron Spelling went into fix-it mode, hiring British B-movie sex bomb Joan Collins to play Blake's vindictive ex-wife, Alexis. Like Venus rising from the foam, a new TV deity was born—a bitch goddess who plotted to alternately destroy or recapture Blake (and lay total waste to the annoyingly saccharine Krystle). How low would Alexis go? To our delight, the pit was bottomless. Just as tennis fans savor Wimbledon, *Dynasty* devotees thrilled to the annual Krystle-Alexis hair pullers: They battled everywhere, from mud ponds to beauty parlors. ✦ *Dynasty* fever raged well into the mid-1980s, and before you could say Nolan Miller, a bevy of celebs with dwindling Q-ratings—Ali MacGraw, George Hamilton, and Rock Hudson, among others—were jumping aboard. What made the whole twisted tangle so hilarious was the writers' struggle to justify cast additions by making them long-lost relatives, like Diahann Carroll as Blake's nefarious half-sister, Dominique Deveraux. Plotlines grew ever more convoluted to accommodate the bloated cast, the stories slipping from heavy-breathing melodrama to cartoonville. (Who could forget the wedding in Moldavia crashed by machine-gun-firing revolutionaries?) ✦ By the late 1980s, with *thirtysomething* self-flagellation in vogue, not even another catfight could forestall the network ax. With Krystle in a coma, Blake shot, and Alexis flying off a balcony, *Dynasty* closed out its decade bereft of dignity. As was only fitting. —NB

MELROSE PLACE

THE ADDRESS WAS 222 SINFUL

BEFORE YOU SIGN THE LEASE at 4616 Melrose Place, you need to understand a few house rules: (1) No parking. This may be L.A., but you'll never see anyone in a car here, unless it's to mow down a cheating husband. (2) No swimming in the pool. Catfights or suicides only. (3) There's a laundry room, but it doesn't seem to be used a lot. ✦ And that's a problem, because anyone hanging around with this bunch long enough is going to get good and dirty. Backstabbing. Conniving. Whoring. Treachery. Adultery. Murder. Complete, 180-degree personality transformations. All crammed into one hour. It's enough to make *Beverly Hills 90210*—the none-too-squeaky-clean sister zip code whence this show spun—seem like an after-school special. ✦ Of course, Fox's *Melrose* would never have become the lurid mélange of broken dreams, shattered promises, and collagen lips that we know so well were it not for Heather Locklear, the hard-hearted blond who took up residence after the first season, sending once-flaccid ratings as high as her hemline. With "special guest stars" like these, who needs enemies? Then again, with enemies like these—and rest assured that everyone on this show, even mild-mannered Matt, is an enemy—who needs *Friends*? ✦ And with such voluminous sudsiness—a highly competitive ad agency, a highly competitive hospital, a highly competitive design business, and a cast of apartment dwellers who would never think to move out (even after one of them tries to blow it up)—who needs a laundry room? —ALEXANDRA JACOBS

TY

S ON AIR 1981–89

IELSEN CHARTING 1st
-85)

S WON 1

NAL TITLE *Oil*

NAL CASTING Sophia
was the first choice for
second-choice Collins–
for camp fare like *The*
nitially turned it down.

OPPORTUNITY BITCHERY
the first African-American woman to star in a sitcom (1968's *Julia*), lobbied for a *Dynasty* role. "I want to be the first black bitch on television," she said. She was.

MASTERPIECE THEATRE IT WASN'T Series creator Esther Shapiro said *Dynasty*'s characters were based on *I, Claudius*.

WHAT PRICE NASTINESS? Each episode cost $1.2 million (weekly wardrobe budget: $10,000).

CAMEOS Ex-President Gerald Ford, his wife, Betty, and former Secretary of State Henry Kissinger

MELROSE PLACE

YEARS ON AIR 1992–present

TOP NIELSEN CHARTING 58th (1996–97)

EMMYS WON 0

HOME BASED Creator Darren Star is said to have been inspired by real-life goings-on at his West Hollywood apartment complex a short distance from L.A.'s actual Melrose Place.

ADD EXEC Locklear was originally signed for only four episodes as Amanda Woodward, but she gave such a boost to the ratings that she became a permanent fixture.

ACCENTED PERFORMANCE Amy Locane's Sandy Louise Harling (who appeared only during the first season) had a come-and-go Southern twang.

CAMEOS Ex-underage porn star Traci Lords as a sexy terrorist

ORDER IN THE COURT Jurors in the O.J. Simpson trial said *Melrose* was one of the shows they "couldn't live without."

JUST THE FACTS

J U S T T H E F A C T S

THE MUNSTERS

YEARS ON AIR 1964–1966

TOP NIELSEN CHARTING 18th (1964–65)

EMMYS WON 0

CAST REUNION Gwynne and Lewis had previously teamed on *Car 54, Where Are You?*

GREAT MINDS THINK ALIKE Lewis has been quoted as saying that he signed on to *The Munsters* because it was "the first original idea to hit television in 15 years." However, *The Addams Family* premiered six days earlier.

LOOKING FOR A HAUNT Producers searched L.A. and the Midwest looking for a dilapidated mansion. When they couldn't find one, they built a house on the studio lot and artificially "aged" it.

ROAD KILLERS The Munster Koach was built by the same man who later built the Batmobile.

LIVING COLOR Though the show was in black and white, the actors still wore odd-colored makeup.

THE BRADY BUNCH

YEARS ON AIR 1969–74

TOP NIELSEN CHARTING 33rd (1971–72)

EMMYS WON 0

WHERE THEY GOT THE IDEA Creator Sherwood Schwartz had read in 1966 that between 20 and 30 percent of all families include kids from previous marriages.

ORIGINAL TITLE *The Brady Brood*

ORIGINAL CASTING Schwartz considered casting Ge Hackman as Mr. Brad was thought too unkn

IMMODEST PROPOSA show never addressec pened to Carol's first h And Schwartz remains she was TV's first divo

POP ART Reed thoug episode in which Gre the line "Oh no! Tomo graduation.... And I've orange hair!" so stupi initially refused to app

THE MUNSTERS

THERE WAS A HALCYON PERIOD in TV history—after *The Adventures of Ozzie & Harriet* but before *The Brady Bunch*—when America scoffed at such nuclear-family perfection. Suddenly, weird was in, and TV families were made up of aliens (*My Favorite Martian*), sorcerers (*Bewitched*), and monsters aplenty. Some may have preferred the absurdist, arch *Addams Family*—but for pure check-your-brain-at-the-door laughs, give us *The Munsters.* ✦ Producers Joe Connelly and Bob Mosher (ironically, alumni of *Leave It to Beaver*) assembled CBS' Munster clan from a Whitman's sampler of horror-movie archetypes and dropped them down in the unsuspecting town of Mockingbird Heights. The running gag was that the amiable Munsters could never understand what it was about them that frightened their neighbors right out of their shoes (sometimes literally). ✦ After all, underneath her Vampira-like glamour, Yvonne DeCarlo's Lily was really a loving mom ("Now, Eddie, go on up to bed. And don't forget to close the lid"), and Butch Patrick's wolf-boy Eddie was oddly endearing as the ultimate school-yard outcast. But it was Fred Gwynne's Frankenstein-esque Herman and his household nemesis, Al Lewis' bloodsucking Grandpa, who got the biggest laughs. Herman was a naive, cowardly concoction of spare parts (when he complained of having "two left feet," he meant it), sharing his dungeon with a crotchety father-in-law who seemed more a product of the borscht belt than his native Transylvania. Sure, they seemed the stuff of nightmares—but their sublime sparring is what prime-time dreams are made of. —MIKE FLAHERTY

EVERY NIGHT WAS HALLOWEEN AS THIS FAMILY OF MISFIT MONSTERS SCARED UP THE LAUGHS

BLAND AMBITION: WE ALL WANTED TO BE PART OF THESE STEPFORD-LIKE LIVES

OK, HERE'S THE STORY: It's 1969. The Vietnam conflict is boiling over, the sexual revolution is gaining steam, and the Manson family is dropping in on Sharon Tate. And then Mike, Carol, and their polite and well-adjusted brood arrive to tell an anxious nation, "Don't worry, guys—everything's going to be just super." As it turns out, that's just what we wanted to hear: With a beloved piece of pop-culture foolishness on ABC titled *The Brady Bunch,* we could blissfully inhabit a peaceful and utopian universe we all knew didn't exist. ✦ The Bradys were two impossibly loving

parents (shag-haired Florence Henderson and Brillo-headed Robert Reed, arguably the grooviest couple in TV history) and six likable kids who each embodied a childhood phase: Marcia the Self-Absorbed (Maureen McCormack), Jan the Overshadowed (Eve Plumb), Cindy the Nosy (Susan Olsen), Bobby the Vulnerable (Mike Lookinland), Peter the Awkward (Christopher Knight), and Greg the Cocky (Barry Williams). Their fatal flaws got the kids in minor trouble (Greg's cigarette excursion, Marcia's humbling *Romeo and Juliet* demotion, Jan's lemons-as-freckle-remover fiasco), but each episode brought new versions of the same lesson: You're great just the way you are. ✦ Since 1974, the show has lived on in after-school syndication, giving new generations of latchkey kids a surrogate—and almost unbearably perfect—family to cling to. Sure, they had bad hair, their clothes were god-awful, and the whole series reeked of camp, but our love affair with *The Brady Bunch* continues today because of the show's devotion to one invaluable tenet: It's hip to be square. —KRISTEN BALDWIN

JUST THE FACTS

THE BEVERLY HILLBILLIES

YEARS ON AIR 1962–71

TOP NIELSEN CHARTING 1st (1962–63, 1963–64)

EMMYS WON 0

FINE-TUNING THE CONCEPT The Clampetts were originally going to move from the country to New York, but creator Paul Henning decided that Beverly Hills was "just as classy." It was also cheaper to shoot the show there.

KEEPING IT IN THE FAMILY? Only Jed and Elly May were actually Clampetts: Granny was Jed's mother-in-law, and Jethro (who's last name was Bodine) was Elly May's second cousin

SHE DIDN'T GER HERS When Nancy Kulp (Miss Hathaway) ran for Congress from Pennsylvania during the 1980s, the right-leaning Ebsen volunteered to campaign against her. She lost.

PRE-ROMAN ERA Sharon Tate appeared as bank secretary Janet Trego during the 1963–64 season.

GREEN ACRES

YEARS ON AIR 1965–71

TOP NIELSEN CHARTING 6th (1966–67)

EMMYS WON 0

ORIGINAL CASTING Anybody but Gabor. CBS programming honcho James Aubrey was concerned her thick accent would be an audience turnoff; a producer convinced him otherwise, citing Desi Arnaz.

HAM ACTING Arnold was played by a succession of porcine performers—most of them female, because lady pigs were easier to manage.

REAL-LIFE INSPIRATION Mr. Haney was loosely based on Col. Tom Parker (Elvis Presley's manager), whom actor Pat Buttram had known decades earlier when Parker was a carnival barker.

HUH? Albert once said of *Green Acres*: "The comedy is like *Pickwick Papers*, or *Gulliver's Travels*, or Voltaire. It's so far out that it becomes truth, deep truth."

HE BEVERLY HILLBILLIES

BACKWOODS SAVVY AND CORNPONE CHARM MADE THE CLAMPETT CLAN AMERICA'S YOKEL HEROES

IT WASN'T HIP, it wasn't topical.... Heck, it was barely literate. But from the start, *The Beverly Hillbillies* was as hot as a hound dog in the sun. When the Hillbillies—accidental oil baron Jed Clampett (Buddy Ebsen), feisty Granny (Irene Ryan), bodacious Elly May (Donna Douglas), and thick-as-a-plank Jethro (Max Baer Jr.)—loaded up their truck and moved to Beverly (Hills, that is), they became like the Joad family played for laughs. ✦ Horrified critics hurled cow pies, but the show made TV history in its nine-year run: It flew to No. 1 within three weeks of its debut—a feat still unmatched—and remained at the top spot for two years. Even more astonishing, the eight most-watched half-hour shows ever are all *Hillbillies* episodes (and all aired in the early months of 1964, in the wake of JFK's assassination). Clearly, for a national psyche bruised by social unrest, civil rights, and Vietnam, the *Hillbillies* acted as a sort of balm. ✦ What was their secret? Mainly, it was the Will Rogers-like charm of these populist heroes—notably ex-song-and-dance man Ebsen and irascible bag of bones Ryan. Jed and his kinfolk always seemed to find ways to confound their rich neighbors, using plain ol' Ozark know-how (and sometimes a heapin' helpin' of Granny's possom-belly stew). So popular were they that *Hillbillies* helped spawn an entire genre of fish-out-of-water shows (including *Green Acres*, which moved the city folk to the boonies) and was canceled only when CBS execs tired of the whole rubes-in-paradise idea, axing *Hillbillies, Acres, Petticoat Junction,* and *Mayberry R.F.D.* Country folk, it seemed, had had their day in the sun. —JOE NEUMAIER/PHOTOGRAPH BY RICHARD HEWETT

GREEN ACRES

FOR THOSE WHO understand the loopy appeal of *Green Acres*, no explanation of the show's greatness is necessary; for those who don't, none is possible. Arguably the most surreal sitcom ever produced, the series counts among its many fans *The Simpsons* creator Matt Groening, who has said, "The bizarre ridiculousness that operates just under the surface of normalcy is what *The Simpsons* and *Green Acres* have in common." ✦ The premise was simple: Big-city lawyer Oliver Wendell Douglas (Eddie Albert) leaves the rat race behind to live the life of a gentleman farmer in rural Hooterville, dragging his ditzy Hungarian wife, Lisa (Eva Gabor), along with him. Once ensconced on the dilapidated farm, though, Oliver finds that Hooterville is populated with strange individuals who operate outside the laws of logic, keeping him in a perpetual state of frazzlement. Among them: lovable con man Mr. Haney (Pat Buttram), who sold Oliver the farm and was continually hawking some dubious piece of useless merchandise; addled county agent Hank Kimball (Alvy Moore), who could find a way to complicate a simple "good morning"; and Arnold Ziffel, the (literal) pig whose grunts could be understood perfectly by everyone except

Oliver. ✦ Lisa, as it turned out, fit into the fabric of Hooterville far better than her hapless husband, who never quite got the hang of the when-in-Rome thing. *Green Acres* took a Kafkaesque concept and turned it into Dada-ish burlesque, and fans ate it up: The absurdist comedy maintained a top 20 spot in the yearly averages for most of its run. Ahead of its time? Out of time—and wholly unique—is more like it. —TS

MAKE ROOM FOR DADA: THIS WACKY TALE WAS THE SURREAL DEAL

ADDITIONAL CREDITS

TOC *p. 2*: Top to bottom: Danny DeVito (ABC, Inc.); Ed Sullivan, John Lennon, Ringo Starr, Paul McCartney (CBS Photo Archive); Pat Sajak, Vanna White (Globe Photos) *p. 3*: Top to bottom: George Clooney, Anthony Edwards (Lauren Greenfield/Sygma); Carol Burnett and supporting cast (CBS Photo Archive); Jaclyn Smith, Farrah Fawcett-Majors, Kate Jackson (ABC, Inc.) *p. 4*: Mary Tyler Moore, Dick Van Dyke (CBS Photo Archive) TOP 20 SHOWS *p. 9*: Mary Tyler Moore (Everett Collection) *p. 10*: Left to right: Michael Richards, Jason Alexander, Julia Louis-Dreyfus, Jerry Seinfeld (Julie Dennis) *p. 13*: Carroll O'Connor, Jean Stapleton (CBS Photo Archive) *pp. 14-15*: Left to right: Woody Harrelson, Kirstie Alley, John Ratzenberger, Rhea Perlman, George Wendt, Ted Danson, Bebe Neuwirth (Tony Costa/Outline) *p. 17*: David Duchovny, Gillian Anderson (Outline) *p. 18*: Lucille Ball, Mary Wickes (Loomis Dean/*Life*) *pp. 20-21*: Left: Ellen DeGeneres; Right: Garry Shandling, Carol Burnett (Gail Albert Halaban) *p. 22*: Joe Spano, Bruce Weitz (Globe Photos) *p. 25*: Johnny Carson, James Brown (Arthur Schatz) *p. 26*: Marge and Homer Simpson (Matt Groening/© TM 20th Century Fox Film Corp. All rights reserved 1992/MPTV) *pp. 28-29*: Left to right: Jackie Gleason, Art Carney, Audrey Meadows, Joyce Randolph (CBS Photo Archive) *pp. 30-31*: Alan Alda, Wayne Rogers (Bill Eppridge) *p. 33*: Leonard Nimoy, William Shatner (Ken Whitmore/MPTV) *p. 34*: Ed Sullivan and showgirl (Allan Grant) *pp. 36-37*: Burgess Meredith (CBS Photo Archive); inset, Rod Serling (Everett Collection) *p. 38*: James Arness (CBS Photo Archive) *pp. 38-39*: Left to right: Morley Safer, Dan Rather, Mike Wallace, Don Hewitt (CBS Photo Archive) *p. 41*: Roseanne, John Goodman (ABC, Inc.) *p. 42*: Larry Hagman (Barry Staver) *p. 43*: Big Bird (Foto Fantasies) COMEDIES *p. 47*: Left to right: Jane Leeves, John Mahoney, Peri Gilpin, Kelsey Grammer, David Hyde Pierce (NBC) *p. 48*: Fred Savage (Bob D'Amico/ABC, Inc.) *p. 49*: Jerry Mathers (Bob Willoughby) *p. 50*: Left to right: Edward Villella, Jack Klugman, Tony Randall (ABC, Inc.) *p. 51*: Bud Abbott, Lou Costello (NBC/Globe Photos) *p. 52*: Howdy Doody (NBC) *p. 53*: Rocky and friends (Everett Collection) *p. 54*: Isabel Sanford, Sherman Hemsley (The Kobal Collection) *p. 55*: Ricky, Ozzie, Harriet, and David Nelson (ABC, Inc.) *p. 56*: Left to right: LaWanda Page, Redd Foxx, Demond Wilson, Whitman Mayo (NBC/Globe Photos) *p. 57*: Ron Howard, Andy Griffith (The Kobal Collection) *p. 58*: Left to right: Ron Carey, James Gregory, Abe Vigoda, Ron Glass, Jack Soo, Hal Linden, Max Gail (ABC, Inc.) *pp. 58-59*: Left: Judd Hirsch, Christopher Lloyd, Marilu Henner; Right: Danny DeVito, Tony Danza (ABC, Inc.) *p. 60*: Clockwise from bottom left: Doris Roberts, Brad Garrett, Ray Romano, Peter Boyle, Patricia Heaton (Jim Wright/Icon International) *p. 61*: Maurice Evans, Elizabeth Montgomery, Dick Sargent (ABC, Inc.) *pp. 62-63*: Left to right: Jerry Paris, Dick Van Dyke, Sheldon Leonard (with glasses), Carl Reiner, Mary Tyler Moore (Allan Grant) *p. 63*: Matt LeBlanc, Courteney Cox, Jennifer Aniston, Matthew Perry, Lisa Kudrow, David Schwimmer (Andrew Eccles/NBC) *p. 64*: Mel Blanc, Jack Benny (CBS Photo Archive) *p. 65*: Bob Newhart (Globe Photos) *p. 66*: Keshia Knight Pulliam, Bill Cosby (NBC/Globe Photos) *p. 67*: The *Monty Python's Flying Circus* troupe (The Kobal Collection) *p. 68*: Michael Gross, Michael J. Fox (NBC/Globe Photos) *p. 69*: Louise Lasser, Mary Kay Place, Debralee Scott, Dody Goodman (Globe Photos) GAME SHOWS *p. 70*: Alex Trebek (Everett Collection) *p. 71*: Top to bottom: Richard Dawson and contestants (ABC, Inc.); Groucho Marx (Photofest) DRAMAS *p. 75*: David Janssen (ABC, Inc.) *p. 76*: Bruce Willis, Cybill Shepherd (ABC, Inc.) *p. 77*: Foreground: left, Patrick Macnee, Diana Rigg (ABC, Inc.) *p. 78*: Telly Savalas (CBS Photo Archive) *p. 79*: Tyne Daly, Sharon Gless (CBS Photo Archive) *p. 80*: Philip Michael Thomas, Don Johnson (Gary Null/NBC) *p. 81*: Tom Selleck (CBS Photo Archive) *p. 83*: Raymond Burr (CBS Photo Archive) *p. 84*: Front row, left to right: Ed Nelson, Dorothy Malone, Warren Anderson, Barbara Parkins, Ryan O'Neal, Mia Farrow; back row: Mary Anderson, Paul Langton (ABC, Inc.) *p. 85*: Alfred Hitchcock (CBS Photo Archive) *p. 86*: Helen Mirren (The Kobal Collection) *p. 87*: Benjamin Bratt, Jerry Orbach (Paul Drinkwater/NBC) *p. 88*: Richard Chamberlain (Everett Collection) *p. 89*: Peter Falk (Everett Collection) *p. 90*: Kristy McNichol (ABC, Inc.) *p. 91*: Ken Olin, Mel Harris (Jim Shea/ABC, Inc.) *p. 92*: Jack Webb (Globe Photos) *p. 93*: Bill Cosby, Robert Culp (Allan Grant) *pp. 94-95*: Left to right: Laura Innes, Anthony Edwards, Julianna Margulies, George Clooney, Eriq LaSalle, Noah Wyle (Lara Jo Regan) *p. 96*: Kyle MacLachlan, Michael Ontkean (Craig Sjodin/ABC, Inc.) *p. 97*: Peter Graves (CBS Photo Archive) *p. 98*: Left to right: Melissa Gilbert, Michael Landon, Karen Grassle, Sidney Greenbush, Melissa Sue Anderson (Photofest) *p. 99*: Left to right: Kami Cotler, Eric Scott, Michael Learned, Ralph Waite, Judy Norton-Taylor (CBS Photo Archive) *p. 100*: Dennis Franz, Jimmy Smits (Michael Ginsburg/ABC, Inc.) *p. 101*: Reed Diamond, Andre Braugher (Larry Fink) *p. 102*: James Garner, Ben Gage (Jon Brenneis/*Life*) *p. 103*: Chuck Connors (ABC, Inc.) *p. 104*: Harry Hamlin, Susan Dey (Globe Photos) *p. 105*: Left to right : Denzel Washington, Ed Flanders, Ed Begley Jr. (Bud Gray/MPTV) *p. 106*: Ken Wahl, William Russ (The Kobal Collection) *p. 107*: James Garner, Noah Beery Jr. (MPTV) *p. 108*: Clint Eastwood (CBS Photo Archive) *p. 109*: Left to right: Michael Landon, Dan Blocker, Lorne Greene (Paul Seligman) MINISERIES *p. 110*: Richard Chamberlain, Rachel Ward (Everett Collection) *p. 111*: *Winds of War*: Robert Mitchum (Shooting Star); *V*: Frank Ashmore, Jane Badler (Photofest); *The Singing Detective* (Photofest) *p. 112*: *Rich Man, Poor Man*: Nick Nolte, Susan Blakely, Peter Strauss (Photofest); *Roots:* LeVar Burton (The Kobal Collection) *p. 113*: Robert Duvall, Tommy Lee Jones (Photofest) TALK/VARIETY *p. 117*: John Belushi (Edie Baskin/Outline) *p. 118*: Carol Burnett (CBS Photo Archive) *p. 119*: Goldie Hawn (NBC/Globe Photos) *p. 120*: Dave Garroway (Philippe Halsman © Halsman Estate) *p. 121*: Howard Morris, Sid Caesar, Imogene Coca, Carl Reiner (Leonard McCombe/Life) *p. 122*: Demi Moore, David Letterman (CBS Photo Archive) *p. 123*: Left to right: Andrea Martin, Joe Flaherty, John Candy, Martin Short, Eugene Levy (NBC/Globe Photos) *p. 124*: Oprah Winfrey (Charles Bennett/AP) *p. 125*: Ernie Kovacs (Archive Photos) GUILTY PLEASURES *p. 129*: Left to right: Farrah Fawcett-Majors, Kate Jackson, Jaclyn Smith (ABC, Inc.) *p. 130*: Billy Mumy, Jonathan Harris (CBS Photo Archive) *p. 131*: Bob Denver (CBS Photo Archive) *p. 132*: Left to right: Ian Ziering, Gabrielle Carteris, Brian Austin Green, Tori Spelling, Shannen Doherty, Jason Priestley, Jennie Garth, Luke Perry (Mikel Roberts/Sygma) *p. 133*: Left to right: Donny Most, Anson Williams, Ron Howard, Henry Winkler (ABC, Inc.) *p. 134*: Left to right: Clarence Williams III, Peggy Lipton, Tige Andrews, Michael Cole (ABC, Inc.) *p. 135*: Jack Lord (CBS Photo Archive) *p. 136*: Adam West, Yvonne Craig (Kurt Gunther/MPTV) *p. 137*: Clayton Moore (ABC, Inc.) *p. 138*: Linda Evans, Joan Collins (ABC, Inc.) *p. 139*: Front row, left to right: Kristin Davis, Andrew Shue, Heather Locklear, Courtney Thorne-Smith, Daphne Zuniga, Josie Bissett, Grant Show, Laura Leighton, Patrick Muldoon; back row: Doug Savant, Thomas Calabro, Marcia Cross, Jack Wagner (Fox/MPTV) *p. 140*: Fred Gwynne (CBS Photo Archive) *p. 141*: Left to right: Mike Lookinland, Christopher Knight, Barry Williams, Maureen McCormick, Eve Plumb, Susan Olsen (Everett Collection) *p. 142*: Clockwise from bottom left: Buddy Ebsen, Donna Douglas, Irene Ryan, Max Baer Jr. (Richard Hewitt/Globe Photos) *p. 143*: Eddie Albert, Eva Gabor (CBS Photo Archive) *This page*: Leonard McCombe/*Life* OPENERS Photographs by Nola López. Comedies: *Taxi* (ABC, Inc.); *The Odd Couple* (ABC, Inc.); *Bewitched* (Everett Collection); *The Bob Newhart Show* (Globe Photos); *Leave It to Beaver* (Everett Collection); *The Dick Van Dyke Show* (Photofest), center (Gabi Rona/MPTV). Dramas: *Miami Vice* (The Kobal Collection); *Mission: Impossible* (Globe Photos). Variety Shows: *Saturday Night Live* (Globe Photos); *Today*–Jane Pauley, Tom Brokaw (Photofest); *Today*–Barbara Walters, Hugh Downs (Photofest) HARDBACK COVER *I Love Lucy* (Philippe Halsman © Halsman Estate); *All in the Family* (Gabi Rona/CBS/MPTV) PAPERBACK COVER *The Mary Tyler Moore Show* (Globe Photos); *Seinfeld* (Julie Dennis); *Star Trek* (NBC/Globe Photos); *The Tonight Show* (Everett Collection); *The Cosby Show* (The Kobal Collection); *thirtysomething* (Everett Collection); *The X-Files* (Mark Seliger/Fox); *Charlie's Angels* (Bruce McBroom/MPTV)